Critical Guides to Spanish Texts

This book is due for return on or before the last date shown below.

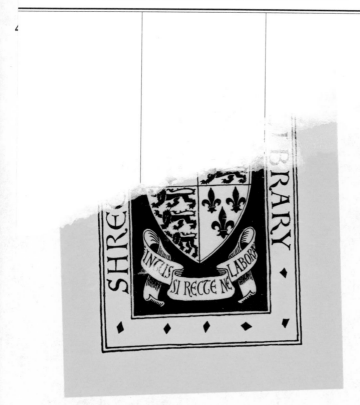

Critical Guides to Spanish Texts

EDITED BY J.E. VAREY AND A.D. DEYERMOND

QUIROGA

Cuentos de amor de locura y de muerte

Peter R. Beardsell

Senior Lecturer in Spanish
University of Sheffield

Grant & Cutler Ltd *in association with*
Tamesis Books Ltd 1986

© Grant & Cutler Ltd
1986

Library of Congress Cataloging-in-Publication Data

Beardsell, Peter R., 1940-
  Quiroga, Cuentos de amor, de locura y de muerte.

  (Critical guides to Spanish texts: 44)
  Bibliography: p.
  Includes index.
  1. Quiroga, Horacio, 1878-1937. Cuentos de amor, de locura y de muerte.
I. Title. II. Series.
PQ8519.Q5C834 1986   863   86-14812
ISBN 0-7293-0247-4 (pbk.)

I.S.B.N. 84-599-1631-6

DEPÓSITO LEGAL: V. 1.819 - 1986

Printed in Spain by
Artes Gráficas Soler, S.A., Valencia
for
GRANT & CUTLER LTD
55-57, GREAT MARLBOROUGH STREET, LONDON W1V 2AY
and
27, SOUTH MAIN STREET, WOLFEBORO, NH 03894-2069, USA

Contents

Contents

Preface

References to the text of *Cuentos de amor de locura y de muerte* are based on the edition authorized for the Biblioteca Clásica y Contemporánea, Editorial Losada, SA, Buenos Aires, 1954, with pagination corresponding to the 17th edition, 1981, indicated in parentheses thus: (p.7). The figures in parentheses in italic type refer to the numbered items in the Bibliographical Note; where necessary these are followed by volume and page numbers, thus: (*19*, p.93).

Instead of taking the fifteen stories in turn — a method suitable for elucidating complex works — I have approached the whole collection by themes, grouping in each chapter three or four representative stories and analysing them in such a way as to draw out the given topic. The last two chapters adopt a more comprehensive method. In order to permit quick reference to pages on individual stories I include an Index at the end of the book.

I have pleasure in acknowledging the generous assistance of the University of Sheffield Research Fund and the British Academy, whose grants enabled me to conduct research on this topic in Montevideo and Buenos Aires in 1983. My thanks are due also to Sra Mireya Callejas and the staff at the Instituto Nacional de Investigaciones y Archivos Literarios in the Biblioteca Nacional, Montevideo, and to Sra Martha J. Barbato and the staff at the Instituto de Literatura Argentina, Buenos Aires.

1. Buenos Aires and Misiones

The collection

Cuentos de amor de locura y de muerte is without doubt Quiroga's most eye-catching title. It is possibly not the best title since the Ancient Egyptians' *Tales of the Magicians*, but it is as alluring as Edgar Allan Poe's *Tales of the Grotesque and Arabesque* (1840), and slightly more refined than Ricardo Güiraldes's *Cuentos de muerte y de sangre*, which appeared in Buenos Aires in 1915, two years before Quiroga's book. It has the virtue of whetting the appetite while at the same time reflecting some — though not all — of the book's contents. The absence from the title of any comma is the result of instructions issued to his publisher (Manuel Gálvez), perhaps to create a non-conformist effect, perhaps to suggest that love, madness and death do not exist as separate items but overlap or combine in any given story.

One of the striking features of this collection is its heterogeneous character. Romance, adventure, fantasy, mystery, murder, horror, madness, social tension, wild country, the struggles of the pioneer, the behaviour of men confronted by imminent death — these are some of the elements. Almost as varied are the dates of composition. The earliest story was first published in 1906 and the last in the same year in which the book appeared. It was not until 1916 that Quiroga gave serious thought to the business of collecting his best stories from the past decade in one volume. But in that period he had published one hundred stories in magazines and newspapers, and even a savage pruning would have left too many. In the event, therefore, the selected material appeared in four volumes: *Cuentos de amor de locura y de muerte* (1917), *Cuentos de la selva (para niños)* (1918), *El salvaje* (1920), and *Anaconda* (1921). Only the book for children has a homogeneity of theme; the others reflect

the wide scope of Quiroga's topics, compensating for what
might be regarded as their lack of artistic unity by an augmented
range of interest among the reading public. It must always be
remembered that the stories were composed for publication first
in magazines and newspapers. Not until *Los desterrados* (1926)
did he seek to produce a collection uniform in style and cohesive
in subject matter.

The following are the eighteen stories in the first editions of
Cuentos de amor de locura y de muerte (Cooperativa Editorial
'Buenos Aires', 1917, repr. 1918) in the order in which Quiroga
originally arranged them, and with the date and magazine or
newspaper of their previous publication. From the third edition
onwards the three stories marked with an asterisk were excluded.

Una estación de amor	
(Un sueño de amor)	*Caras y Caretas*, 13 Jan. 1912
Los ojos sombríos*	*Caras y Caretas*, 15 Apr. 1911
El solitario	*Fray Mocho*, 30 May 1913
La muerte de Isolda	*Fray Mocho*, 29 May 1914
El infierno artificial*	*Fray Mocho*, 4 Apr. 1913
La gallina degollada	*Caras y Caretas*, 10 Jul. 1909
Los buques suicidantes	*Caras y Caretas*, 27 Oct. 1906
El almohadón de plumas	*Caras y Caretas*, 13 Jul. 1907
El perro rabioso*	*Caras y Caretas*, 1 Oct. 1910
A la deriva	*Fray Mocho*, 7 Jun. 1912
La insolación	*Caras y Caretas*, 7 Mar. 1908
El alambre de púa	*Fray Mocho*, 23 Aug. 1912
Los mensú	*Fray Mocho*, 3 Apr. 1914
Yaguaí	*Fray Mocho*, 26 Dec. 1913
Los pescadores de vigas	*Fray Mocho*, 2 May 1913
La miel silvestre	*Caras y Caretas*, 20 Mar. 1909
Nuestro primer cigarro	
(El cigarro pateador)	*Fray Mocho*, 24 Jan. 1913
La meningitis y su sombra	Not previously published

The magazines and the social background in Buenos Aires

One of the factors contributing to Quiroga's concentration on
the short story as a form of literary expression was the avail-

ability of a regular outlet in magazines in Buenos Aires. In his correspondence we find ample evidence that much of his income derived from payments for articles and stories. Until he made a name for himself he had been heavily dependent on school teaching and the help of friends and relatives. But in the year 1906 he appears to have made a break-through: 'Por aquí voy mejorando visiblemente', he wrote to a friend. 'Resulta que *Caras y Caretas*, fuera de los cuentos que les agradan mucho, me han pedido *notas* para ser ilustradas con fotografías ...Por cada una de estas notas me dan $30, y 20 por cada cuento. Como podrá aparecer uno de cada uno por mes, son $50 útiles' (*12*, II, p.113). When he moved away from Buenos Aires in 1910 he relinquished his teacher's stipend, and in January 1911 he wrote: 'Vivo exclusivamente de la pluma, y C. y C. me paga ahora $40 por página' (*12*, II, p.140). Eventually he was appointed Justice of the Peace and Civil Registry Officer for the district of San Ignacio (Misiones), at a salary of 150 pesos per month. To this he could add the meagre takings from the sale of fruit and vegetables from his land, but even then his writing earned a substantial proportion of his income. Since he had the unusual habit of recording the fee paid for each of his stories we know that the average was about 120 pesos per story (though 'Una estación de amor' earned as much as 300). Between 1910 and 1916, when he moved back to Buenos Aires, he published thirty-four stories at an average of one every two months or so, besides a great number of articles. It is impossible to believe that he did not adapt his production in some respect to the kind of market on which his livelihood depended.

During his most productive and successful years (1906-26) Quiroga often published in prestigious Buenos Aires newspapers such as *La Nación*, *El Hogar*, *Crítica* and *La Prensa*. But two magazines were the first vehicles for all but one of the *Cuentos de amor de locura y de muerte*: from 1906 *Caras y Caretas* and from 1912 *Fray Mocho*. The European fashion for illustrated magazines began in 1898 with the founding of *Caras y Caretas*. It described itself as a 'Semanario festivo, literario, artístico y de actualidades' (exactly the words used later by *Fray Mocho*). Number 458 (13 July 1907), which contains Quiroga's 'El

almohadón de plumas', is typical. On the cover a political
cartoon satirizes a forthcoming Conference; inside, a second
cartoon pursues the theme, mocking the tendency to create large
groups and hold conferences; a third cartoon ridicules direct
taxation and tax inspectors; and a caricature of a politician
further illustrates the moderately liberal politics of the
magazine. There are photographs, with captions, of banquets,
Independence Day celebrations and other social events. Several
pages illustrate the news from Italy, France, Spain and Great
Britain (an air crash, a wine crisis, a royal visit, Venice in danger
of sinking into the water, etc.). On other pages we find articles
on sport (horse racing), an art exhibition, and fruit trees. And
scattered through the magazine the following literary items: a
poem by Manuel Ugarte ('La ausencia'), a review of Leopoldo
Lugones's book of *modernista* verse, *Los crepúsculos del jardín*,
and short stories by Emilio Vera González ('El final del
cuento'), Antonio Sánchez Ruiz ('Misterios del anarquismo'),
Leopoldo Lugones ('El hombre muerto') and Quiroga himself.

It is clear from this outline of the typical contents of *Caras y
Caretas* (and *Fray Mocho*, though slimmer, was essentially the
same kind of publication) that the magazine was catering for an
extremely varied taste among its readers. Consistently, however,
it avoided deep and detailed analysis, and attributed high
importance to the entertainment of its readers while at the same
time informing them, stimulating their interest, and offering
them brief samples of culture. The usual level of literary
contributions is well represented by Lugones's 'El hombre
muerto'. It is a fantasy in which a man claims to be dead and
wishes everyone to acknowledge that his death is a fact; people
merely think him mad until one morning they lift his blanket and
discover him lying there, nothing but dry bones. It does not bear
comparison with Quiroga's own story with the same title,
written fourteen years later and collected in *Los desterrados*. But
Quiroga's 'El almohadón de plumas' does not look out of place
here, provided that we give it no more than superficial attention.
Quiroga's possible allusions to the world of vampires and his
sensational ending make the right kind of appeal to readers
nurtured on the vogue for fantasy. However, his story blends

elegant form and evocative mood with those elements, so that it actually enhances the quality of this issue of the magazine. It is not difficult to understand why he was by then winning a growing popularity among the readers.

One further useful indication of the readership may be found in the type of advertisement placed in *Caras y Caretas* (and again *Fray Mocho* is similar). In number 458 the following items are advertised in the forty-two pages preceding the title page: motor cars and horse-drawn carriages; records, pianos, clocks, jewellery, and fashions for clothes; soap and perfume; tea, cognac, anís and wine; cough mixture, health drinks and drugs, a dental clinic; and farming equipment ('Para los estancieros', according to one advertisement). The readers, then, were thought likely to buy luxury goods and items to improve their appearance, their health and the general quality of life. They were not short of money; some, indeed, were large landowners. Cosmopolitan, sophisticated, amenable to both liberal and conservative attitudes, they were upper and middle-class people in a city pulsating with growth, vitality and change.

Buenos Aires already had a population of over one million in those years. The majority of the inhabitants had been born in Europe: immigration, especially from Italy and Spain, was not only swelling the numbers but intensifying the European cultural orientation and sharpening the political awareness. Although the government was still controlled by the landowning oligarchy through the Partido Autonomista Nacional, the growing middle class was clamouring for participation, and the working class was agitating for reforms. This opposition found its most successful expression at that time through the Unión Cívica Radical. Acts of revolutionary violence in 1905 failed to shake the ruling group, but by 1912 the threat of the Radicals (who abstained from voting in the 1910 elections for tactical reasons) caused the new Conservative President, Roque Sáenz Peña, to introduce certain liberalizing measures, such as the law for compulsory suffrage by secret ballot for every male over the age of eighteen. Radical and Socialist representation in government at both local and congressional level therefore greatly expanded. In the elections of 1916 it was the Radical, Hipólito Yrigoyen, who was victorious, and the country continued under Radical governments until the end of the golden era and the beginning of military intervention in 1930.

Meanwhile Argentina was enjoying what is described by historians as a period of economic prosperity — a prosperity reflected notably in the resplendent life styles of the upper crust of society, and in the bright opportunities beckoning the middle classes. Buenos Aires's architecture helped to give the city something of the air of Paris or London. In relation to the rest of Latin America it became a cultural centre. Theatre and concert audiences gained a reputation for good taste, many publishing houses prospered, and the literacy rate was the highest in the Hispanic world. On the other hand it must be recognized that in relation to the world's greatest cultural centres Buenos Aires was still found to be backward and frustrating by a number of writers. The novelist Manuel Gálvez, for example, complained that people in general were uninterested in the arts, and that theatre-going was chiefly a social event; the public was easily scandalized by experiment or honest comment, which meant that the writer's freedom was severely restricted; and cultural contact with Europe was difficult. He also found fault with 'la vanidad y superficialidad del ambiente'.[1] Ricardo Güiraldes wrote, even more aggressively, 'Estoy cansado de esta ciudad sin alma, de este burdel de puerto en que sólo se festejan el oro y los chistes de mala entraña.'[2] In short, there were complaints of excessive materialism and triviality.

It was indeed extremely difficult for a writer to live for his art alone, experimenting, following artistic inspiration, and ignoring public response. Quiroga could never forget the need to earn a living, and his view of short-story writing as one means of doing so meant some degree of reconciliation with the prevailing conditions. But much the same might be said of other great short-story writers, such as France's Guy de Maupassant, who once referred to his art as 'des lignes que je vends le plus cher

[1] Manuel Gálvez, *La Argentina en nuestros libros* (Santiago: Editorial Ercilla, 1935), p.22.

[2] *Obras completas* (Buenos Aires: Losada, 1962), p.767.

possible', and 'ce métier abominable'.[3] Compromise of this kind may sometimes influence the content, and certainly influences the length and structure, but it does not necessarily determine the merit of a short story. There is compromise too in magazines like *Caras y Caretas* and *Fray Mocho*. Although pitched at a less exclusive intellectual level than the purely literary reviews, they played an important role in stimulating the arts. Their relatively wide circulation, long life (*Caras y Caretas* lasted until 1939) and considerable prestige testify to the interest in current affairs, general knowledge and culture among a fair number of the population.

Misiones

Far from being the slave of society, Quiroga was notorious for his nonconformity. He is remembered as an introvert, inclined to be moody, unsociable and authoritarian (though honest, loyal and capable of great friendship).[4] He was also a man of enterprise, imagination and a sense of adventure. Flashbacks to his youth in Uruguay would illustrate these characteristics entertainingly, but there is ample evidence in the years when he was composing the *Cuentos de amor de locura y de muerte*, for this includes the first period when he temporarily abandoned Buenos Aires for a life in the wild country.

Only five of the stories in the collection are set in the city. Many of the rest take place in the remote province of Misiones, an area in the north-east of Argentina thrusting like a finger between the Rivers Paraná and Uruguay as far north as the Iguazú Falls, with Paraguay to one side and Brazil to the other. In the sixteenth and seventeenth centuries Jesuit priests set up missions in this subtropical territory, and taught the indigenous people new types of agriculture. After the expulsion of the Jesuits the region declined and the buildings fell into ruins.

[3] 'Lines that I sell at the highest possible price' and 'this wretched trade'. *Œuvres complètes de Guy de Maupassant* (Paris: Conard, 1908), p.lvii.

[4] The texts of interviews with Enrique Amorim, Jorge Lenoble and Marcos Kaner — all of whom knew Quiroga personally — are documents D336, D337.1, and D337.2 in the Archivo Horacio Quiroga, Instituto Nacional de Investigaciones y Archivos Literarios, Montevideo.

In 1903 an archeological expedition was commissioned to study these sites, and Quiroga managed to have his name included as the party's official photographer. At the beginning of the expedition he proved ill-equipped to cope with the conditions, but by the time he returned to Buenos Aires he was a changed man. No longer fussy about his dress, he often adopted a taciturn air on social occasions, and felt a deep disillusionment with his literary accomplishment, which led him gradually to eliminate the affectation in his writing and to seek a greater variety of subjects. Several short stories and articles were to reflect this experience of the city man's discovery of the wild country.

Not many months after his return to Buenos Aires, Quiroga heard of the opportunities offered to cotton growers in the Chaco, an enormous plain extending from the northern reaches of the pampa into Paraguay. With the remainder of his inheritance he purchased land on the banks of the River Saladito, twenty miles south of Resistencia, built his own house, and set about converting seventeen acres into a cotton plantation. Economically the enterprise was a total failure, mainly because of his inept handling of the local casual labourers and the early arrival of rains, but also because he would often spend time on extravagant ideas at the expense of those details essential to economic viability. After that year in the Chaco he returned penniless to Buenos Aires, but the experience had proved a vitally important — and satisfying — exercise in effort and self-sufficiency, and it was later to inspire a handful of short stories (one of which was 'La insolación').

Two years after this, in 1906, Quiroga decided to take advantage of the Argentinian government's favourable terms for settlers willing to develop the cultivation of *yerba mate* (Paraguayan tea) in Misiones. He acquired 457 acres near San Ignacio, and chose a plateau overlooking the River Paraná as the site for his future home. For a while it was the scene of his holidays, but in 1910, immediately after his first marriage, he moved there to live in the bungalow that he had built himself. Only yards away was the forest, where he cut tracks to facilitate hunting, one of his favourite occupations. Animal skins adorned the inside walls of his bungalow, and outside he kept a small zoo of birds, deer, monkeys, alligators and a tiger. In his garden he grew a variety of flowers and shrubs, and on a larger scale he produced cassava, bananas, oranges, pineapples and other fruit. During these years he embarked on a number of bold, innovative, but often impractical ventures: a partnership to grow *yerba mate*, a factory for the manufacture of charcoal, a small oven for ceramics, and projects involving maize, tar, honey, resin and dye. Before long the *yerba mate* partnership was wound up, the charcoal factory eventually burnt down, and the other enterprises sooner or later caved in, but the Quiroga who, as a youth, had nearly blown up his chemistry workshop was clearly indulging a natural trait and fulfilling a vital need.

Meanwhile Quiroga's domestic life was inevitably showing the impact of his aspirations as a pioneer. Arguing that childbirth was no more than a perfectly natural biological process, he insisted on his first child being born in the bungalow with no outside help. That is how his daughter, Eglé, was delivered in 1911. A year later his son, Darío, was born (in hospital). Once the two children were old enough he took them with him on hunts in the forest and trips on the river, with the idea that rather than shelter them he should expose them to situations where they might learn to understand danger without fearing it. Although genuinely fond of his wife, he proved a difficult man to live with: strong-willed, tyrannical, susceptible to stormy outbursts as well as to tender moods. By 1915 the family quarrels became increasingly frequent, with an unexpected and tragic result: Ana María took her own life. A little over a year later, with the onset of economic problems and his children's education to provide for, Quiroga moved back to Buenos Aires. He was to live in Misiones again, with his second wife, from 1932 to 1936, but until then his contact with the area came through holidays.

'*Modernismo*', '*criollismo*', *Horacio Quiroga*

In Buenos Aires he was able to establish a closer contact with the literary world. During the last seven years he had received no intimation of the public's reaction to the Misiones theme beyond

the fact that his stories were readily accepted by the magazines
and newspapers in the capital. He had recognized them as being
something of an innovation; only on his return did he learn how
highly they were regarded.

Years previously, in the Uruguayan town of Salto (where he
was born in 1878), Quiroga had experimented with verse as well
as prose. At the end of the century, in Montevideo, he led a
small group of literary eccentrics known as the 'Consistorio del
Gay Saber' (the name is that of a medieval poetic academy),
which gained the reputation of introducing his country to
modernismo. This term applies to the literary trends prevalent in
Hispanic literature approximately from 1890 to 1915, a culmination of tendencies with their source of inspiration chiefly in
France. The Parnassian aspect emphasized beauty of form and
expression; vivid colours, the exquisite, the ornate, the
picturesque; exotic, legendary and mythological themes.
Symbolist influences encouraged the expression of intimate
thoughts and emotions; a belief in correspondences between the
writer's own senses and images or symbols in the world of
nature, in equivalences among the characteristics of the different
senses, and in the writer's visionary perception of the mystical,
full reality of things; the use of language seeking vague,
mysterious or obscure effect through mere suggestion, and
language producing musical effects. The Decadent aspect was
experimentation with technique and language; an apparent
mental and spiritual degeneration; and the use of irony and
burlesque. And in addition to these foreign influences one
belonging to the New World gained strength in the later part of
the period: the glorification of indigenous Latin American
traditions and realities.

Quiroga's literary initiation was especially along the lines of
the Decadent aspect of *modernismo*. *Los arrecifes de coral*
(1901) — a collection of verse, poetic prose and short stories —
represents the best of his production from the years in Uruguay,
but they are works of experimentation and, to be frank, literary
immaturity. The period of *modernismo*, which in Buenos Aires
had fully begun in 1896 with Rubén Darío's visit to the city, was
already approaching its end when Quiroga wrote the earliest of

the *Cuentos de amor de locura y de muerte*, and the avant-garde made no more than increasingly frequent splutters from 1911 before exploding into life in 1921 with Jorge Luis Borges's return from Europe.

Important though the Europeanizing aspect of the literary scene undoubtedly was, the background to *Cuentos de amor de locura y de muerte* — and in particular to those stories on Misiones topics — can be fully understood only when the New World aspect is taken into account. In ideological terms Argentina had usually tended to associate Europe with the forces of civilization, enlightenment and progress, and the Latin American territories with negative forces such as barbarism, ignorance and backwardness. While cosmopolitan Buenos Aires represented the former, the vast and untamed hinterland had seemed to threaten the latter. However, just as there had always been politicians advocating less dominance of the country by the principal city (and it was late in the nineteenth century before Buenos Aires was formally recognized as the capital), there had long been writers intent on affirming an independent national literature by describing the natural environment, examining the life of local inhabitants, and sometimes even using a form of Spanish heavily influenced by rustic speech. This development embraced nineteenth-century *cuadros de costumbres* (sketches of local customs) and *literatura gauchesca* (books about gauchos in semi-gaucho language). Although it often overlapped with the European-based developments in realism and naturalism, its focus sometimes became so local that the label 'Regionalism' has been used for it (particularly in the years 1910 to 1929). Another factor was the reaction to the tide of immigrants by Argentina's *criollos* (people of direct European descent but born in Argentina). Needing a sense of national identity, *criollo* writers explored and exalted their own traditions and values, usually choosing rural themes and settings, and abandoning the excesses of *modernismo* in favour of a greater simplicity of expression and a closer relationship between language and the regional theme.

In historical perspective Quiroga's Misiones (and Chaco) stories have been considered an important contribution to

criollo literature. They help in the literary exploration of
Argentinian territory, they are rural, they exalt *criollo* values
such as virility and endurance, and they are narrated in a
language that is functional rather than ornamental. It is difficult
to confine Quiroga to *criollismo*, however. Too idiosyncratic to
conform to any single trend, he was aware only that he was
breaking new ground and that Misiones, with its settlers,
animals, climate and landscape, was a remote and exotic subject
matter for his city readers. In his stories — whether or not they
are set in Misiones — many elements are blended, including the
social habits of his magazine readers, both *criollo* and cosmopolitan, and the influences of his favourite short-story writers,
all of whom were foreign: Rudyard Kipling, Guy de
Maupassant, and Edgar Allan Poe. 'Sin género de duda
provengo de estos hombres', he confessed in 1936, the year
before his death (*12*, I, p.72). But at his best he was unique. He
wrote almost two hundred stories, in addition to scores of
articles, two novels, a play and a film script (which was never
used). Critical opinion agrees that his best work is to be found in
books of the period 1917 to 1926. *Cuentos de amor de locura y
de muerte* emerges therefore as a collection containing both the
more vigorous youthful aspects of his writing and the more
sober features of his plenitude.

2. Love

Three of the *Cuentos de amor de locura y de muerte* may be classed as love stories: 'Una estación de amor', 'La muerte de Isolda', and 'La meningitis y su sombra'. In three other stories love is a subsidiary theme, the marriage of the protagonists forming an important background to the main action: 'El solitario', 'La gallina degollada', and 'El almohadón de plumas'. In distributing love stories in approximately this proportion among most of his volumes, Quiroga appears to have been keeping in mind the need to achieve some kind of balance in the material. But his two novels, *Historia de un amor turbio* (which appeared in 1908) and *Pasado amor* (1929), add strong support to the belief that he wrote on the theme of love not merely in order to entertain but in response to psychological stimuli with their basis in reality.

Quiroga was highly sensitive to the physical attractions of women. Once considered a dandy, he retained a tendency to flirtatiousness even when he became less fastidious about his appearance. His private correspondence amply and entertainingly demonstrates this trait. It reveals, for example, how he spent an hour playing with the foot of a sixteen-year-old girl during dinner (*12*, II, p.99). And it includes letters to a friend in which he wrote bad verse to express his erotic fantasies. Whatever he may have achieved by means of flirtations, however, his important amorous experiences invariably ended in frustration or failure. The most notorious of these was the romance that inspired 'Una estación de amor'. In the carnival of 1898 in Salto, Uruguay, Quiroga was captivated by the attractive María Esther Jurkowski. He ignored the gossip about the irregularities in María Esther's household (her mother was not married to Jurkowski), and courted the girl assiduously. But her family, disliking Quiroga and regarding his prospects as inauspicious, foiled a planned elopement, and dispatched the girl to Buenos Aires. Quiroga was profoundly distressed; seven years later, still tormented by her memory, he discovered where she lived and visited her a few times. The years had wrought changes in both of them (María Esther, according to some sources, had become addicted to drugs), and they soon parted again, with disillusionment and pain (*12*, II, pp.92, 95). One of the conspicuous aspects of Quiroga's romantic life was his tendency to fall in love with women much younger than himself. In 1908 it was one of his school pupils, Ana María Cirés. After a series of crises the two were married on 30 December 1909. As we observed in the previous chapter, the marriage was tender at times but grew increasingly tempestuous. His wife's suicide in 1915 obviously produced a profound impact on his outlook and gave him further cause to develop the sense that barriers repeatedly prevented him from achieving happiness through love. It is worth noting that the two other great loves in his life confirmed this pattern. In 1925 his tenacious courtship of another teenager was foiled by the girl's even more determined parents. Not long after this, in 1927, Quiroga married his daughter's friend, María Elena Bravo; but she was twenty years old and he was forty-nine, their interests and their temperaments were different, and neither their daughter (born in 1928) nor their move to Misiones (in 1932) was enough to prevent María Elena's discontentment and their eventual separation.

Although these biographical details are probably more relevant than any literary models, it is fairly clear that Poe and Dostoyevsky exerted important influences on the erotic theme in Quiroga. As Margo Clantz has demonstrated (*19*, p.110), he shared Poe's fascination with morbidity, incest and child heroines, and Dostoyevsky's fascination with women's flightiness, childlike innocence, and the mixture of lasciviousness and chastity. It will be noticed that some of these elements come into play in the stories discussed below, while others belong more aptly to the study of the macabre in Chapter 3.

In his stories Quiroga almost invariably adopted the male standpoint. The use of a first-person narrator in two of the love stories of *Cuentos de amor de locura y de muerte* eliminates our ability as readers to know what the female characters think or feel. But even in 'Una estación de amor' the third-person narrative produces precisely the same results, requiring us to guess Lidia's reactions while actually informing us of Nébel's. Another of the salient features that these three stories have in common is the powerful effect of the girl's physical attractiveness on the protagonist. In 'Una estación de amor' Quiroga makes no delay before stressing the features that appeal to Nébel: Lidia's extreme youthfulness; the whiteness of the girl's skin, constrasting with the darkness of her hair and eyelashes; and — with more lingering detail — the girl's eyes. The narrative concentrates our attention on those eyes, not only because they enhance her beauty but because they are momentarily directed at Nébel. In other words, it is not only a question of their attractiveness as objects but of their active role in producing an emotional effect on the man. Nébel, we read, 'quedó deslumbrado' (p.7), and from that moment he is captivated, charmed or (we might almost say) bewitched by the young girl. We find these same ingredients on the opening page of 'La muerte de Isolda': the woman's youth, the beauty expressed through the paleness of her skin and 'la perfecta solidaridad de mirada, boca, cuello, modo de entrecerrar los ojos' (p.35), and the seductive power of that 'cuerpo hermoso'. Believing her eyes to be directed at him, the narrator experiences 'el más adorable sueño de amor que haya tenido nunca' (p.35).[5] Similarly, in 'La meningitis y su sombra' Durán immediately feels the effects caused by the girl's eyes, lovingly fixed on his own (p.140).

These stories treat love as initially a matter of sexual attraction, in which youth, beauty and bewitching eyes all play their part. It is noticeable that both male and female seem to be playing roles created for them by society, and that flirtation is openly practised. The protagonist of 'La muerte de Isolda' remarks blandly that, although courting Inés, 'yo vivía en una esfera de mundo donde me era inevitable flirtear...' (p.37). He has no success when flirting with one girl, and 'En consecuencia flirteé con amiga suya...'. In this tale of love wasted through

[5] 'Los ojos sombríos' (a story included in the first two editions of *Cuentos de amor de locura y de muerte*) is another case where even the narrator is captivated by the heroine's eyes.

neglect, foolishness and failure to understand true values, there is no doubt that flirtation is an important detrimental factor. We can not conclude, however, that Quiroga wished to expose it as a vice, since in 'La meningitis y su sombra' María Elvira's flirting is regarded as a social asset ('flirtea admirablemente cuantas veces se lo proponen'; p.150) with no harmful effect on the development of true love and no disapproval by the man who is in love with her. In 'Una estación de amor' Nébel's immediate response to Lida's attractiveness is a form of flirtation, but it develops into a serious courtship. We may therefore infer that Quiroga was simply reflecting social behaviour that he and his readers knew well and regarded as mischievous fun.

A few of the love stories in Quiroga's other collections are romantic idylls in which an improbable situation leads to a perfect love and a happy ending. One called 'Un idilio' (*El salvaje*) involves a case where the protagonist is asked by a friend to stand in for him at his wedding ceremony. The role of bridegroom is to be only temporary, but this fictitious romance becomes a real love between the protagonist and his friend's bride. A successful outcome for them both is facilitated by the convenient death of the friend. 'La meningitis y su sombra' has an important feature in common with 'Un idilio': from an unreal love a real one is nurtured. The sombre gravity of illness does not weigh heavily, even at the beginning, and it is not long before events infuse the story with the happy innocence of an idyll. In the other two love stories of our collection there is an idyllic phase through which the relationship passes: 'Este fue el principio de un idilio que duró tres meses' (p.8), 'La quería mucho, y ella, inmensamente a mí' (p.37). At the same time there is in both of these stories an element which lifts the events temporarily above the level of humdrum reality. In 'La muerte de Isolda' the scene of the narrator's own idyll is an opera house during a performance of Wagner's *Tristan and Isolde*. There is clearly an interplay between fiction and reality, the opera's action (and its passion) having in certain respects both a parallel and an antithesis in Padilla's tale. But the point that concerns us here is the special situation created for the audience during a dramatic performance, an atmosphere in which fantasy may assume unusual proportions. The first narrator's brief idyll is made possible by this setting. Much the same may be said of 'Una estación de amor', where an idyll is made possible by the freedom of expression in a carnival atmosphere. Quiroga recognized the universal wish for love to be idyllic. Where 'La meningitis y su sombra' differs from the other two stories is in the fact that it stays within the realm of idylls whereas the other two soon fall into a bitter reality.

Powerful emotions abound in Quiroga's love stories: 'Nébel llegó al más alto grado de pasión...' (p.9), '...surgía sangrando la desolación de haberla perdido' (p.41), '...mi cabeza era un vértigo vivo, con locos impulsos de saltar al aire y lanzar alaridos de felicidad' (p.143). In fact, the male protagonists are at times so overwhelmed that love can envelop the whole of their attention and sway the course of their lives. Nébel twice contemplates suicide, Durán decides to leave the country, and Padilla leaves Buenos Aires for eight years. There are even moments of sentimentality and melodrama, as at the end of 'La muerte de Isolda': the opera's background of Wagnerian passion, Padilla's sense of facing a crucial moment in his destiny, Inés sobbing violently with the awareness of lost happiness, a reminder that ten years of their lives have passed, and the emotional final words echoing the past and ringing with pain and regret: '—No, no... ¡Es demasiado tarde!...' (p.42).

Although these male protagonists are quickly overwhelmed by their emotions, their love is handled with a fair degree of complexity. The most notable of the three cases is that of Padilla, who explains his psychological problem as follows: 'Hice cuanto estuvo en mí para que fuera mía. La quería mucho, y ella, inmensamente a mí. Por esto cedió un día, y desde ese instante, privado de tensión, mi amor se enfrió' (p.37). In Padilla sexual desire so dominates the first stage of his love for Inés that once it is satisfied nothing else seems to remain, and he turns to other women for more sexual conquests. Only when Inés has ceased to belong to him, only when she is again unattainable, does he recognize that his love for her has not ended. The central scene in this story is that of the rupture of their relations, where Padilla — with the advantage of hindsight — draws attention to the self-destructive impulses that seize him: a perverseness of the kind Quiroga surely noticed in the writings of Poe.[6] Padilla's 'profundo disgusto de mí mismo' (p.38) only leads him to more extreme behaviour. His offended pride increases his aggression. And an awareness of the damage he is causing only worsens his treatment of Inés: 'Sentí el vértigo de enlodarme más aún.' Significantly, his jibes are about their love-making. Having behaved so outrageously, Padilla is then filled with remorse, desperation and humiliation. But he senses that the damage is irreparable, and Inés's reply '¡Es demasiado tarde!' merely confirms his instinct.

In the light of this scene the story as a whole suggests that a happy course in the love between a man and a woman can be prevented by a failure to recognize lasting value and a failure to control destructive impulses. Another of the main factors, however, seems to be pre-marital sexual intercourse. In 'Una estación de amor' the adolescent Nébel's desire for Lidia is less powerful than the psychological need to maintain her virginity until they are married. Alone with her one evening, neither kissing nor touching her, he feels in the presence of 'un amor inmaculado, que tan fácil le habría sido manchar. ¡Pero luego, una vez su mujer!' (p.15). Even when Lidia's mother creates the perfect opportunity for uninterrupted love-making Nébel resists for the sake of 'un amor puro en toda su aureola de poético idilio' (p.18). Eleven years later, when he eventually sleeps with her, the predominant psychological reaction is that of destroying a pure memory, and bitterness mixes with his regret. Intrinsically connected with this destruction of purity, brought about by sexual intercourse, is the destruction of an idyllic memory, which is caused by the ravaging effects of time, with changing fortunes and contaminating experience: 'Nébel lo había guardado, ese recuerdo sin mancha, pureza inmaculada de sus dieciocho años, y que ahora yacía allí, enfangado hasta el

[6] Poe's narrator in 'The Imp of the Perverse' explains a tendency 'to do wrong for the wrong's sake', 'an innate and primitive principle of human action, a paradoxical something, which we may call *perverseness*, for want of a more characteristic term. Through its promptings we act... for the reason that we should *not*... The assurance of the wrong or error of any action is often the one unconquerable *force* which impels us' (*Tales of Adventure Mystery and Imagination*, 3rd ed. London: Ward, Lock, 1891, pp.298-99).

cáliz, sobre una cama de sirvienta' (p.26). These are sentiments closely analogous to those of Padilla, who cherishes the memory of 'un primer amor, con todo el encanto dignificante que un idilio virginal tiene para el hombre hecho, que después amó cien veces' (p.40). Quiroga seems to imply the innate need to retain a pure, idyllic memory of love, but he simultaneously reveals the tendency for such idylls to be sullied.

Psychological barriers are therefore fundamental to the theme of these stories. But social obstacles also play their part, the notorious instance being that of 'Una estación de amor'. What intervenes in an idyllic relationship is the external factor of the social acceptability of the girl's family. Although it is not a matter of concern to either of the lovers, it is predominant in the parents. Nébel's father refuses to sanction his family's union with a household whose moral standing is low, whereas Lidia's mother desires to enhance her family's social status at all cost. Motivated by the urge to humiliate the society that has treated her with scorn, she plans her daughter's sexual conquest in order to make the marriage enforcible and to place Nébel's family in the same moral standing as her own. It is her failure that leads to the end of the courtship. Quiroga seems to have a mixed attitude to the mother. On the one hand he clearly despises her readiness to sacrifice her daughter. On the other hand he recognizes some justice in her complaint against the hypocrisy of people like Nébel's father, who has slept with his partner before marriage and made his fortune at the expense of his clients. Ultimately it is society as a whole, rather than the mother or father individually, that is censured.[7]

The detrimental effect of social attitudes is marginally less in 'La muerte de Isolda', but it is one of the factors weighing on Padilla's mind. 'Nuestro ambiente social era distinto', he recalls (p.37), and disparagingly he remarks that Inés's mother would have permitted her daughter's love-making 'para no perder la más vaga posibilidad de subir con su hija a una esfera más alta' (p.37). Padilla's search for conquests besides Inés is connected with his own social ambition. Although it does not constitute a

[7] The drama *Las sacrificadas* (1920), which is a reworking of the same material, places even greater emphasis on these social obstacles to the romance.

barrier in 'La meningitis y su sombra', the question of social acceptability certainly arises. María Elvira's family suffer a sense of indignity through her amorous feelings for a virtual stranger, but it is made clear that the situation would be far worse if the man in her hallucinations were 'un sujeto cualquiera de insuficiente posición social' (p.135). It is one more indication that Quiroga saw social prejudices as a constant threat to love.

If we now take into consideration the three stories in which love constitutes an important subsidiary theme we find an over-whelmingly negative view. Each one shows the failure of a married relationship. In 'El solitario' a basic incompatibility between Kassim and his wife, María, is compounded by the man's inadequacy and the woman's greed and ambition. It is in these psychological causes that we must find one explanation for the murder, although perhaps María's taunting cry of 'cornudo' (p.33) hints at the crucial motivation. In 'La gallina degollada' Mazzini and Berta need to express their love for each other through having children, but are placed under repeated and unendurable stress through the idiocy of the first four (and the slaughter of the fifth). Quarrels break out in which each partner seeks to cast off a sense of guilt by blaming the other for the hereditary cause of their children's mental illness (syphilitic meningitis from Mazzini's father or tubercular meningitis from Berta's side). What Quiroga leaves us with, however, is the impression that one way or another — by means of external or internal forces — the marriage is doomed to suffer destructive blows. Despite the element of fantasy in 'El almohadón de plumas' there is a similar overall impression of a marriage destined to end in some kind of failure. Jordán is hard, cold, impassive and taciturn; Alicia is timid and delicate; they marry in autumn, and the girl's adolescent dreams of love are rapidly destroyed. In other words, there is a clear invitation for us to find some connection between Alicia's marriage and her coldness, listlessness, illness and death. Although the explanation we are finally given casts the blame on an external agent, we can not fail to ponder on the coincidence whereby the girl's decline begins immediately after her marriage. In per-spective, then, none of the three stories suggests any bright prospects for a marriage. Whether by failings within the partners themselves or by outside forces which intrude in the relationship, the marriages all bring ultimate misery.

This impression confirms the conclusions to which two of the love stories lead. Love constantly meets barriers, sometimes internal barriers such as the cooling of sexual desire or the underestimate of a partner's worth, sometimes external barriers such as social differences or parental interference. There is a tendency for time to exert a tarnishing effect, for idyllic love to be sullied, and for events to turn sour. It is significant that in the exception to this pattern — 'La meningitis y su sombra' — love commences purely as fiction, and the borders between delusion, role playing, and reality remain indistinct until the last pages: a story, in other words, which always seems to have a greater connection with day-dreaming than with lived experience.

3. Madness and the Macabre

In *Cuentos de amor de locura y de muerte* every tale of madness is also a tale of horror, of love, or of death. The term 'locura' applies equally well to mental illness (i.e. pathological madness) and to rash, impulsive or ill-judged acts. Two of the stories — 'La gallina degollada' and 'La meningitis y su sombra' — present indubitable cases of subnormal or impaired minds, where the condition manifests itself as a symptom of a disease. A few others offer more veiled cases, where the border between abnormality and normality (or normality under stress) remains unclear. Is it madness that causes a man unexpectedly to murder his wife in 'El solitario', causes the members of a ship's crew to commit suicide in 'Los buques suicidantes', and torments a young woman with hallucinations in 'El almohadón de plumas'? The enquiry deserves to be taken this far, although I do not include here several instances of human behaviour that many people would regard as rash, impulsive or ill-judged, such as míster Jones's strenuous activity beneath a sweltering sun ('La insolación'), Candiyú's risk with a river in flood merely to earn himself a luxury ('Los pescadores de vigas'), and Padilla's destruction of his own love and happiness ('La muerte de Isolda'). The emphasis, therefore, lies heavily on madness as a pathological state.[8]

Pathological madness

'La gallina degollada' illustrates the effect that macabre

---

[8] An avid reader of Dostoyevsky, Quiroga once described *The Idiot* and *The Possessed* as 'lo más profundo... que se haya escrito en lengua humana' (*12*, II, p.89). Although this inevitably points to a general influence of the Russian novelist on Quiroga's use of abnormal psychology as a literary theme, we notice little attempt to reproduce Dostoyevsky's profundity. On the other hand the Uruguayan considered Dostoyevsky to be of all nineteenth-century novelists 'sobre todo, el más *extraño, disparatado* y *absurdo*' (*12*, II, p.88 — Quiroga's own emphasis), and in this aspect there is certainly an affinity.

elements have on what was potentially a psychological tragedy. A couple have seen their first four children lose their sanity at an early age; their remaining sane child now loses her life at the hands of the subnormal children. The story opens with a paragraph describing the physical symptoms of the children's abnormality, firmly fixing our attention on the importance that madness is to have in the subsequent course of events. Quiroga follows this with information indicating their rudimentary, bestial characteristics, and rounds off the opening impression with a compassionate reference to the lack of any maternal care shown for them. He then turns to the background to the disease. In the course of a quarrel illustrating the stress exerted on Mazzini's and Berta's relationship he allows us to discover that the children's madness has been diagnosed as a symptom of meningitis. Since this was a disease endemic in parts of Latin America and not by any means infrequent in his day, Quiroga was choosing a reasonably likely cause for insanity. Moreover, he shows some familiarity with medical diagnosis when he indicates that the meningitis may be the result of congenital syphilis, inherited from Mazzini's father, or of infection from Berta's pulmonary trouble (tuberculosis, presumably).

The next stage in the story is the false alarm when the remaining healthy child, suffering from indigestion, looks as though she may be going the same way as her brothers. It is a timely reminder of the shadow cast by idiocy over this household, and it prepares the way for the four subnormal children to become the story's focal point again. They watch, stupefied, as the servant drains a hen's blood — a scene which appears at the time merely to illustrate the bestial nature of their pleasures. Quiroga is now treating their mental condition not as an illness or a subject for psychological analysis, but as a brutalising force. In other words, he is no longer interested in them primarily as sick children but as creatures reduced to brute instinct and bestiality. The language itself betrays the disposition of the author: he refers to them here as 'los monstruous' and 'las cuatro bestias' (p.49). The scene is set for a climax in which madness converts four human beings into monsters.

During the crucial paragraphs covering the four boys' trans-

ition from their usual state of indifference to the seizure of their
sister Quiroga's handling of madness is not what we might
expect in a psychologically oriented story. Instead of taking us
into the minds of these children, the narrative retains a wholly
external focus. When the boys' gaze, which is fixed on the bricks
and the setting sun, takes into account the arrival of Bertita the
fact is presented to us not subjectively, in terms of a coherent
thought, but impersonally, in terms of an object seen: '...algo se
interpuso entre su mirada y el cerco' (p.49). In the passage that
ensues, the only interpretative indications of their behaviour
come from what any other observer would notice in their
expression: their eyes look on at first with indifference and then
with animation; their pupils gleam; and gradually their whole
faces express a 'sensación de gula bestial'. One final hint at their
motivation is given in subordinate clauses of the narrative,
which remind us that it was in the kitchen 'donde esa mañana se
había desangrado la gallina, bien sujeta, arrancándole la vida
segundo por segundo' (p.50).

Quiroga has certainly given enough information for a few
confident conclusions to be drawn. The children intend to renew
the sensuous pleasure that they had obtained when the hen was
killed. The idea of using Bertita could be suggested to them
merely by circumstances. She arrives at the time when their
senses are aroused by the setting sun, she blocks their view ('se
interpuso'), and she draws attention to her throat ('apoyaba la
garganta sobre la cresta del cerco'). We do not need an insight
into the children's thoughts to realize that sheer sensuality,
instinct, and imitation could explain their behaviour. However,
other possibilities suggest themselves. One is the unspoken erotic
ingredient, capable of producing the 'gula bestial' in the boys'
faces as the girl attempts to climb the wall — an interpretation
which accords with our knowledge that Quiroga had been
interested in the writings of the Marquis de Sade and Leopold
von Sacher-Masoch.[9] But another possibility is the motive of

[9] In 1900 Quiroga and his friend Alberto Brignole published a piece entitled
'Sadismo-Masoquismo' in their own magazine, *Revista del Salto* (and in the
following issue added a clarification to reassure their readers that the
phenomenon was not a vice but a neurosis). As the author of horror stories
Quiroga invites us to join him in a kind of sado-masochistic experience:

revenge. What the author totally fails to tell us is whether the children feel any resentment for their parents' lack of care and affection, whether the resentment is directed in the form of jealousy towards their pampered sister. All he does is to show us how the four brothers are 'brutalmente' pushed away to their bench while the girl is taken for a walk with their parents. Such omissions clearly indicate, of course, that Quiroga had no intention of writing a story in which the psychological motivation of characters would be a focus of interest. In effect, madness here is not a subject investigated in its own right but a means of creating an unusual situation. Madness causes a series of responses culminating in horror. It is not a psychological story but a horror story in which insanity serves as a manifestation of some irresistible force controlling the lives of a family and leading to ruin and tragedy.

The other story with pathological madness at the heart of the action is 'La meningitis y su sombra', and here too it serves mainly as a pretext rather than as a subject for analysis. In the sick mental condition induced apparently by an attack of meningitis a girl believes herself to be in love with a man she has barely met. The role of the disease is to create the strange situation in which this man — who narrates the events — acts the part of a lover in order to restore her health, but gradually finds himself falling genuinely in love with her. In the symptoms of María Elvira's illness Quiroga takes the trouble to present recognizable signs of meningitis: on the first night, a sudden headache with fatigue; the following morning, a fever; from the second night, fever, acute anxiety and prolonged delirium; and after a few days, a slow recovery. Such symptoms are consistent with

identification with a suffering protagonist, fear that such an event might occur to us, and simultaneous awareness, of course, that it is not happening to us, and that we are witnessing the suffering of another person. The combination of eroticism and cruelty is discernible in other stories besides 'La gallina degollada'. For example, the husband who stabs his wife in the heart after baring her breast ('El solitario'); and the bride who spends her solitary hours in bed, where her blood is drained from her as though by her husband ('El almohadón de plumas'). Closely linked with this is the choice of victim in two of the stories: Alicia, a new bride, 'rubia, angelical y tímida', and Bertita, four years old, adored and pampered. They are precisely the right types to accord with that specific aspect of sadism whereby the subject of cruelty or torture is young, tender and loved.

meningococcal meningitis, although it should be noticed that in
most cases of this disease there would also be a stiffness of the
neck, in a quarter of the cases red spots would appear, and in a
large number of cases death would occur within the first week.[10]
But we are now expecting a greater degree of verisimilitude than
Quiroga was interested in creating. It was sufficient for him to
keep in mind simply that meningitis was a frequent threat and
popularly known to produce insanity and delirium. No doubt it
was blamed for many other diseases. Indeed, the doctor in this
story is cautious in his diagnosis: '¿Meningitis? — me dijo —
¡Sabe Dios lo que es! Al principio parecía, y anoche también...
Hoy ya no tenemos idea de lo que será' (p.138).

Having established a plausible reason for María Elvira to
suffer deliriums, Quiroga might have focused on her mind as she
recovered her health. Instead, he chose to concentrate on the
mind of his narrator, Durán, who is increasingly bemused,
becomes uncertain where the border between reality and
unreality lies, and eventually loves her 'como un loco' (p.152).
His own dreams assume the air of hallucinations in which his
role of subordination to María Elvira is expressed through the
images of a formless shadow and a walking thermometer. It is a
story, therefore, where madness, which has already created the
girl's love, looms out of the man's love. Playfully, Quiroga
seems to be hinting that love and madness are inseparable. One
result of the game, in which reality and delusion come face to
face, is the merging of reality with illusion and dream. The
ending of the story, explaining the use of a first-person
narrative, adds an extra dimension — the reader's own level of
reality. However, it is so clearly a wish fulfilment (for the
reader, no doubt, as much as for the narrator) that we are compelled to sense its fictitious, dream-like character.

On the fringe of insanity

With 'El solitario' we come to a quite different phenomenon.
There is no disease to produce mental subnormality or hallucin-

---

[10] See William A.R. Thompson, *Black's Medical Dictionary*, 31st ed. (London:
Adam & Charles Black, 1976), p.546.

atory states, but domestic strife culminating in an act of murder. In using the term 'murder' I imply not only unlawful killing, which is beyond dispute here, but malice aforethought, which the evidence strongly suggests. Having worked until two o'clock in the morning to complete the brooch (or jewelled pin) that he has been commissioned to make — and that his wife longs to possess — Kassim silently enters the bedroom, lights the bedside lamp, walks back to his workshop (to pick up the brooch?), returns to the bedroom, gently opens his wife's nightdress, and plunges the brooch into her heart. Once his wife's body has stopped quivering he walks out, quietly closing the door behind him. It would be difficult to argue that the jeweller acts in the heat of the moment. On the other hand, it might be possible to argue that the incongruous tranquillity of his demeanour contrasting with the violence of his act proves that Kassim's mind has lost its grasp of reality. The case for diminished responsibility would presumably point to the overwhelming effect of his wife's persistent demands for jewellery, submitting his mind to stresses that it could not endure. The evidence for insanity might well be contradicted if we took into account his wife's constant insults against his manliness, crowned by the admission of adultery (in an unguarded moment she cries: 'cornudo', p.33). For this means that Kassim's motive could be the avenging of his offended honour. Moreover, the jewel is a kind of substitute for Kassim's masculinity. When completed, 'el brillante resplandecía firme y varonil en su engarce'; the baring of his wife's breast as a prelude to her death emphasizes the erotic connection. A modern psychiatrist might argue, of course, that this obsessive preoccupation with his sexual inadequacy indicates mental abnormality. Although Quiroga himself was not interested in the legal implications of his story, he was certainly fascinated by the hazy border between sanity and madness represented by such crimes.

In the same story, indeed, he includes another instance of human behaviour on the fringe of insanity. Kassim's wife, passionate, covetous and ambitious by nature, finds her deepest instincts frustrated by marriage. In the course of the story her passions become obsessive, disproportionate, uncontained, and

if we examine the key references to her state of mind we notice
how they hint at a gradual development from normality to
abnormality:

'apasionada'; '¡y con cuánta pasión deseaba ella!'   (p.29)
'Porque su pasión eran las voluminosas piedras';
'Seguía el trabajo con loca hambre'; 'Un ataque de
sollozos'.   (p.30)
'una pasión'; 'con rabioso fastidio'.   (p.31)
'en plena crisis de nervios'; 'los ojos le salían de las
órbitas'; 'enloquecida'.   (p.32)
'Estás enferma, María...'; 'La crisis de nervios retornó';
'alarido'; 'pesadilla'.   (p.33)

It is therefore the second case in 'El solitario' of a natural
human trait getting out of hand.

After madness combined with disease, violence and passion,
we turn briefly to madness and fantasy in 'Los buques
suicidantes'. Quiroga took up the well-known theme of ships
that have been mysteriously abandoned, and offered as one
possible explanation the suicide of all the crew. This behaviour,
described by the passenger who has once survived such a
situation, falls within the scope of madness. The members of
this crew are not aroused from apathy when a fellow sailor
jumps into the sea, but succumb to a pervasive somnambulism
and throw themselves overboard too. A partial indication of the
psychological state of these men is offered. The abandoned ship
creates a 'terror supersticioso' in the sailors (p.53), a frame of
mind aggravated by absolute calm in the air and water. The fear
of dying, the sense that nothing can prevent their death, the
'defensa angustiosa y a *toda costa*' against what they feel — all
this is supposed to have a hypnotic effect on them and to induce
the very result that they dread and resist. The survivor is the only
one to offer no resistance and to accept the hypnotic influence
passively. It amounts to an interesting theory but it is doubtful
whether there is much psychological verisimilitude in it. Quiroga
was more concerned with writing a fantasy in which madness
serves to create the eerie entertainment.

The extent of Quiroga's interest in fantasy and the super-natural is not fully represented in *Cuentos de amor de locura y de muerte*. When pruning the collection for its third edition he eliminated a tale narrated in diary form by a man with rabies who imagines snakes infesting his house, believes that everyone is seeking to kill him, shoots his wife, and is hunted down by neighbours, who discover him in a tree, howling like a wild animal ('El perro rabioso'). Quiroga displayed even greater dis-cretion by eliminating at the same time a story about addiction to cocaine ('El infierno artificial'), in which an addict commits suicide but enters a kind of afterlife. This supernatural dimension dominates the pages: the addict, now a minute figure inside the cranium of a skeleton, calls for cocaine, is found by a gravedigger and, granted his request, becomes transformed into a full-sized person, craving cocaine. I mention these two dis-carded stories in order to emphasize the connection in Quiroga's fiction between madness and a number of ingredients ranging from sheer fantasy to macabre realism.

Hallucinations and the macabre

In 'El almohadón de plumas' the sick protagonist experiences vivid hallucinations.[11] Although it is not a case of complete insanity it is one of temporary states of brain derangement occurring with increasing frequency. The prelude to Alicia's physical deterioration is her shivering in the cold house. She then grows thin, catches influenza, and weakens quickly. An acute case of anemia is diagnosed. Simultaneously with her first physical symptoms we notice the first signs of odd behaviour: she sleeps during all the hours of her husband's absence in order to avoid thinking of anything before his return. But it is in her severely weakened physical state that hallucinations occur. At first they are formless and floating, later they move to the floor level and seem to be associated with the carpet on each side of the bed. Eventually they become sufficiently frightening to awaken her in the night, screaming and perspiring. The most

[11] This is the original form of the title (retained by Losada in the 1954 and subsequent editions). Several later versions have the singular: *pluma*.

persistent of them is a man-like creature on tiptoe on the carpet, staring at her. In the daytime Alicia's condition abates, but each dusk brings a relapse, in which her mind suffers delusions of monsters crawling towards her bed and scrambling up the bed-spread. Two other psychological quirks are worth noting: each morning she awakes to the feeling of an immense weight on top of her; she is unwilling for anyone to touch the bed or tidy her pillow. Finally, she falls into a delirium, and death ensues after two days.

Despite the fact that Quiroga has given us a convincing enough sketch of the physical causes and psychological symptoms of Alicia's derangement, it is, strictly speaking, unnecessary to the plot: a young woman marries, fails to achieve the happy fulfilment of her wishes, and dies through loss of blood. The cause of her anemia is a monster in her pillow which gradually drains her blood through her temples. Yet on various levels the madness — if we may call it such — has a function, always important and in some respects absolutely essential. In the more superficial aspect, Alicia's hallucinations permit Quiroga to insert mysterious, grotesque, frightening and horrific ingredients in the story, so that the spectacularly horrific ending is not without anticipation. These tangible representations of the subconscious help, in other words, to create an atmosphere of mystery and terror. Secondly, the insight into Alicia's mind is a vital means of giving her an identity, of creating a person whose suffering can provoke curiosity and perhaps even compassion in the reader. Thirdly, the mental aberrations exert a profound influence on our interpretation of the story. The key passage concerns a description of Alicia's hallucinations one night. With her eyes staring at the carpet, she cries out for her husband, 'y al verlo aparecer Alicia lanzó un alarido de horror' (p.56). She has confused whatever terrifying thing she imagines on the carpet with the figure of her husband, and it is some time before she is able to distinguish one from the other: 'Alicia lo miró con extravío, miró la alfombra, volvió a mirarlo, y después de largo rato de estupefacta confrontación, se serenó.' It is immediately after this point that Quiroga describes the anthropoid monster in one of her most persistent hallucinations, as though he might be wishing to hint at its connection with Jordán. If this is the case it means that Alicia subconsciously associates her husband with all that terrifies and debilitates her. To put it cautiously first, her life is drained away by the coldness, severity and impassiveness of Jordán, who prevents her from feeling his love for her and causes the destruction of her dreams. At the very least this would literally explain her earliest behaviour, without recourse to the monster in the pillow. In the story as a whole, however, we would have to recognize that the psychological and physical developments occur along parallel lines. Alicia's will to live is drained as her blood is sucked from her, Jordán's treatment of her is matched by the monster's action in her pillow. The monster may be seen, therefore, as a representation in tangible form of the monstrousness of her husband. This has become the interpretation favoured by critics, who agree that Jordán is — figuratively speaking — a human vampire (*27*, pp.115-16; *19*, pp.215-19).

While this thought-provoking interpretation certainly has its justification in the associations incurred by Alicia's mental derangement, it must not blind us to the fact that far more spontaneous and primordial reactions come from any first reading of the story. Let us acknowledge that readers of *Caras y Caretas* in 1907 were not only familiar with vampire stories, but expected to come across them from time to time.[12] Let us recognize, moreover, that Quiroga himself wrote vampire stories (one entitled 'El vampiro' appeared in 1911 and another with the same title in 1927). What this implies is that Quiroga was deliberately encouraging his readers to spot the vampire-like qualities of this story in order to mislead them and increase the shock at the end. It is surely a mistake to underestimate the importance of the parasite in Alicia's pillow — a spectacularly repulsive and surprising explanation of her death which acquires

[12] Critics find Quiroga's interest in vampires to be one of the prominent indications of his debt to Edgar Allan Poe. The extent of Poe's influence on Quiroga's macabre tales undoubtedly ranges from the borrowing of themes to the choice of individual details (see especially Margo Clantz, *19*, pp.93-118). But as Noé Jitrik remarks, in Buenos Aires in those days 'se da todo junto: naturalismo en literatura al principio, psiquiatría, sociología, espiritismo, fantaciencia, literatura fantástica, constituyen el clima en los medios cultos tanto como en los populares' (*23*, p.99).

all the emphasis at the moment the story is completed. Curiously, a creature with some similarity to this was the subject of a Buenos Aires newspaper report twenty-seven years before Quiroga published his story. According to the report, headed 'Un caso raro', a six-year-old girl grew pale and thin, recuperated during a holiday in the country, and had a relapse when she returned. Further deterioration in her condition was prevented by the discovery inside her pillow of 'un bicho, cuyo nombre ignoramos, color negro y de grandes dimensiones, de forma redonda y con varias y largas patas', which had been sucking the girl's blood.[13] There is no evidence that Quiroga knew of this real case, but it helps us to see vividly that his imagination was operating within the bounds of possible reality. What he sought to create was not something wholly fictitious or supernatural but a fantastic exaggeration of the credible. Indeed, his story is especially effective when read at night by people leaning on a feather pillow.

Augmented horror

The horrific quality of 'La gallina degollada' and 'El almohadón de plumas' is intensified, as we have seen, by madness. But Quiroga showed in 'La miel silvestre' how horror could be independent of insanity. The protagonist of this story suffers as a result of foolhardiness and ignorance. Gabriel Benincasa, a public accountant, leaves the city for a holiday in Misiones, where he quickly discovers that exploring and hunting in the bush are not as easy as he had expected. Moreover, in the middle of the second night of his trip the house in which he is staying is raided by carnivorous soldier ants, which his god-father repels using creolin. On the third day Benincasa makes a solitary incursion into the undergrowth. He raids a bees' nest and greedily samples the honey. It is a wild honey with narcotic properties, however, and paralysed through its effect he is incapable of escape or defence when carnivorous ants come to devour him.

[13] *La Prensa*, Buenos Aires, 7 November, 1880, p.1. I owe this information to the article by A. Veiravé, 'El almohadón de plumas. Lo ficticio y lo real' (*19*, pp.209-14).

One of the important features is the careful preparation of the reader in order that the ending should achieve its fullest impact. Numerous warnings and hints are given: the two young cousins whose escapade has a fortunate and gentle outcome, the signs of Benincasa's inexperience and excessive self-confidence (particularly the pride in his *stromboot*), and the arrival of ants during the night.[14] A similar use of foreshadowing will be noticed in 'La gallina degollada': the subnormal children's fascination with the setting sun and flowing blood, their neglect and their sister's pampered treatment, Bertita's interruption of their line of vision, and her chin resting on the wall. As a result of these features the ending of both stories mostly fulfils expectation, the only unforeseen element being the actual form in which the inevitable disaster occurs, and the sheer extent of the horror produced. They are cases where horror derives from augmented disaster. In 'La miel silvestre' — as in 'La gallina degollada' and 'El almohadón de plumas' — we notice a tendency to draw out the suspense and linger over the horror. The failure of the bees to bring about an expected catastrophe turns attention to the honey. Gradually Benincasa's circumstances deteriorate, as his sensations change from gluttonous pleasure to dizziness, a pricking sensation, and paralysis. Worse than this, his thoughts change from curiosity to anxiety, fear, panic and terror. Quiroga enjoys the pun twice introduced into his narrative by the word 'hormiguear', and mocks the protagonist by allowing him to see the connection between his sensations and the ants, before the ants actually arrive and before it dawns on him that they could pose a threat in his present predicament. The author's greatest cruelty, however, is in preserving Benincasa's mental faculties intact. Having rendered him helpless, he now enables him to see the ants approach and be aware of their implication, so that the full horror of events is now apparent not only to us but to the protagonist. His feelings heighten our own; his cry of terror is emitted for us too.

[14] The behaviour of these ants, and ways in which the settler may cope with them, are carefully described in Quiroga's article 'Las hormigas carnívoras de Misiones: la corrección' (*14*, pp.24-28). According to him the term 'corrección' derives from the Brazilian word 'correzón'.

The lingering is perhaps less conspicuous in 'La gallina degollada', but there is still an obvious attempt to relish the growing sense of horror. Every movement of Bertita gradually increases her peril as, little by little, the boys' attitude changes from indifference to interest and then to 'gula bestial', and their actions are transformed from sluggishness to violence. In 'El almohadón de plumas' it is a question of creating a crescendo of mystery and uneasiness, where suspense is underpinned not by a sense of the inevitable but by genuine ignorance of the facts. Bloodstains are seen on the pillow, they resemble insect bites, the maid lifts the pillow to the light but drops it in fright, her fear causes Jordan's hair to stand on end. It will be noticed that here too the culmination of suspense is a cry of horror emitted by one of the characters, a direct communication of emotion from the text to the reader.

All of these deaths are grisly, but two of them are particularly gory events. I am not thinking of 'El solitario', for Kassim's fatal blow is neat and precise. Nor would I include 'El almohadón de plumas' here, for although the idea is extremely macabre, the visual representation of Alicia's death is one of gradual decline rather than an abrupt and violent end. This leaves two stories where the events are so unspeakably horrendous that Quiroga resisted the temptation to commit them to words. In his earlier writing there are sometimes detailed visual descriptions of such scenes, but he seems to have discovered that omission produces better results. To supply full details is to reduce the level of readers' participation, whereas to encourage readers to use their imagination is to draw them into the scene and intensify their emotional responses. Moreover, the absence of details has the effect of creating a psychological shield for the sensitive reader, rather like the protection afforded when we cover or avert our eyes to avoid an offensive sight. It is also a matter of delicacy and subtlety as opposed to heavy-handedness. However, he may be accused of maliciously prompting the imagination to ensure that it operates along the right lines. In 'La gallina degollada', although he does not tell literally what the boys do to their sister, he does make a neat reference to the hen that they had seen killed: 'Uno de ellos le

apretó el cuello, apartando los bucles como si fueran plumas.'
And then with remorseless insistence he adds the gratuitous
reminder, as they drag her off to the kitchen, that it was here
'donde esa mañana se había desangrado la gallina, bien sujeta,
arrancándole la vida segundo por segundo' (p.50). After this the
imagination is guided by the reactions of the girl's parents, for
the horror is increased precisely because it is they who discover
her. It is a similar procedure in 'La miel silvestre', where the
narrative gradually progresses through careful details until it
reaches the precise moment when the gruesome activity begins, a
final reminder of the potential threat is given (instead of using
the term *corrección* Quiroga switches to the more explicit
'hormigas carnívoras'), and then the standpoint changes, veiling
the action itself and transferring to the moment when the
victim's remains are discovered.

'La miel silvestre' differs from 'La gallina degollada',
however, in that it does not end with that discovery. A final
paragraph adds general information about the rarity of wild
honey with a paralysing capability, and its characteristic resin
flavour. There is a practical purpose here. The didactic touch
gives an air of authenticity to the story, as though it were
intended to serve as a warning to any inexperienced adventurers.
It is also ironic: had Benincasa known these facts he would have
survived. 'El almohadón de plumas' has an additional paragraph of this kind, though its didactic air is clearly a playful
pretence contrived to give the reader momentary doubts about
his own pillow. In both cases, however, the last paragraph has
an even more important function than those I have mentioned.
There is a sharp contrast between the high emotions aroused in
us by the macabre events and the cool, detached language with
which the stories end. To some extent the effect is similar to that
achieved by the omission of gory details: a decorous avoidance
of the crude and the sensational. On the other hand this absence
of feeling seems so incongruous, under the circumstances, that it
suggests a callous disregard for human suffering. It produces
therefore a secondary shock which enhances the horror already
aroused by the thought of what the dead person has suffered.
Kassim's dispassionate and meticulous behaviour after he has

murdered his wife has essentially the same result: 'cerrando tras
de sí la puerta sin hacer ruido' (p.34).

Three of the most horrific ideas in all of Quiroga's writings
are found in *Cuentos de amor de locura y de muerte*: the adored
child whose throat is slit by her four mad brothers; the young
accountant who is paralysed and then eaten alive by carnivorous
ants; the delicate bride whose blood is sucked through her
temple by a monstrous parasite living in her pillow. But other
collections also contain macabre stories (written mostly during
the first half of Quiroga's career), and perhaps not surprisingly
he once felt obliged to defend his moral health: 'Creo gozar de
una salud perfecta en lo moral. Aún más: soy un perfecto
burgués, con familia normal y afectos normales' (*27*, p.179). It
was a particularly effective defence, since he was attributing his
own values equally to the society that read his stories. By writing
tales of madness and horror he was, of course, catering for
public taste besides responding to inner obsessions or literary
influences. In general terms the macabre ingredients may be said
to derive from the Decadentism incorporated into Latin
America via *modernismo*. In more specific terms they stem from
Quiroga's early interest in sado-masochism and his absorption
of influences from Edgar Allan Poe. Nothing, however, can
detract from our recognition that Quiroga combined a great
dexterity in the presentation of horrific events with a supremely
powerful imagination. Although there is some justification for
regarding these stories as less informative or thought-provoking
than the tales of death studied in Chapter 4, they are equally
entertaining and equally successful as works of art.

4. Death

'El Dios en que no creo'

Although Quiroga's attitude to death underwent an important change during his last years, his attitude to metaphysics remained essentially constant. As one of his greatest friends of the 1930s put it: 'A Quiroga no le interesaban los dilemas de la metafísica' (*15*, p.16). Other people's God was for him 'el dios en que no creo' (*12*, II, p.84). He wrote a handful of stories on religious topics, always giving a lay interpretation of the events: for example, Christ walking through the cold streets of modern Paris faced with an apparent indifference to His sacrifice ('Jesucristo', in *Los arrecifes de coral*); or Salomé betraying the whereabouts of Jesus — even though she believes Him to be the Messiah — in order to avoid the slaying of babies under the age of two ('Navidad', in *2*). In Quiroga's stories as a whole, therefore, characters faced with danger or aware of imminent death rarely entertain metaphysical thoughts and never approach religious experience. Any solutions to the problems constantly posed by death seem to be available only within life on earth. What counts for him in particular is the way the characters treat their life, the way they cope with dying, and in general their relation to the eternal elements.

All but three of the *Cuentos de amor de locura y de muerte* include a death, and even in the exceptions death provides a poetic background ('La muerte de Isolda') or poses a severe threat ('Los pescadores de vigas', 'La meningitis y su sombra'). It is not entirely satisfactory to attribute this fascination or obsession to literary influences, despite the thematic importance of death for the Decadent poets, and for Poe, Maupassant, Dostoyevsky and Kipling, all of whom were read and admired by Quiroga. For a full explanation we must take into account certain events affecting himself and those around him. Both his father and step-father met unusually violent deaths. The former, leaping ashore during a family outing on the river, struck the edge of the boat with the rifle he was carrying, and shot himself in the chest. Years later his step-father, who had been left half-paralysed by a brain hemorrhage, took his own life with a rifle placed under his chin. But the episode affecting Quiroga most critically involved his friend Federico Ferrando, a member of the 'Consistorio del Gay Saber'. While Quiroga was examining a pistol belonging to his friend, the weapon fired and Ferrando fell dead with a bullet in his mouth. It was the event that led directly to Quiroga's emigration to Buenos Aires. The suicide of his first wife in 1915 and his own suicide in 1937 (after he learned that he had a terminal illness) confirm this pattern of violent deaths.

It is hardly surprising, therefore, that rather than abstract the theme for intellectual consideration, Quiroga's stories tend to treat death as something dramatic, personal, and charged with emotional impact. Moreover, with the fatality usually occurring at or near the end of a story, the narrative's effect is to a large extent controlled by the event. There is one important case of an unexpected death, 'El solitario', where the act of murder encourages a retrospective reassessment of Kassim's character. But in the eight other stories where death has a major significance it is at least partly foreseen, and at the most is fully inevitable: 'La gallina degollada', 'El almohadón de plumas', 'A la deriva', 'La insolación', 'El alambre de púa', 'Yaguaí', 'Los mensú', and 'La miel silvestre'. Each of them consists of a series of events that steadily and remorselessly lead to the fatality. Usually, moreover, it is the death itself that provides the climax. In some stories, of course, it is a macabre event to which we react with horror; the last chapter dealt with those. In this chapter I propose to examine in detail two cases which offer a more serious and more poignant treatment, and then briefly to discuss a story in which death provides a subsidiary theme.

'A la deriva'

The critics, who unanimously regard 'A la deriva' as one of Quiroga's best stories, have drawn attention to its universal qualities. Although the protagonist's Christian name is used once by his wife, the narrative always refers to him with the impersonal 'el hombre' and makes no serious effort to particularize his identity. We know that he lives with his wife Dorotea in a cabin on the banks of the river Paraná, five hours upstream from Tacurú-Pucú, that he carries a machete in his belt, that he has been on bad terms with his nearest neighbour, Alves, that he once worked for a timber company in Tacurú-Pucú owned by a míster Dougald, whom he has not seen for two or three years, that he first met the company's timber buyer, Lorenzo Cubilla, one Thursday in Holy Week, and that he has a friend called Gaona in the town. But that is all, and even that information is imparted indirectly. There is no doubt that Quiroga was attempting to transfer our interest from the man's individual circumstances to his behaviour, and that he was inviting us to use this particular death as a basis for some generalizations. It is easy to carry the argument too far, however. 'A la deriva' is not so much about death as about dying, and especially about one way of dying. By this I do not mean dying by snake-bite but dying with coolness, with supreme effort to survive, and with a determined grasp at every last fragment of hope.

In his article 'Las víboras venenosas del norte', published fifteen months after this story (*14*, p.42), Quiroga refuted the popular belief that Misiones was infested with venomous snakes and remarked how rare it was for any person to see more than ten or fifteen in a year. According to him the *yarará* (*Lachesis lanceolatus*) was the most common, while the *yararacussú* (*Lachesis yararacussú*) was very rare. Curiously, he chose the former in the first version of 'A la deriva', but in the definitive version opted for the rare species as the agent of Paulino's death. The main reason was presumably the fact that this snake combines a deadly venom with an imposing size (one of 1.8 metres had been found in Misiones). But the rarity of the species tends to underline the idea that the protagonist of his story has been exceptionally unlucky. It is clearly a mistake to claim — as some commentators do — that Quiroga intends this event to be regarded as very common and regular in Misiones. What he is stressing here is not the considerable likelihood of a person dying by this means but the fact that a bite by such a snake is, on the whole, an unexpected event. His story begins, therefore, with the implicit warning that there is no place for complacency or unguarded moments, since death can strike any of us at any moment of inattentiveness.

The incident that causes the man's death is confined to two short paragraphs, for Quiroga's main interest lies in the predicament arising after the snake-bite. It is a situation fraught with tension and pathos. A man has a wound that will prove fatal unless it receives prompt medical treatment, but his remote location means that medical attention is inaccessible. Quiroga concentrates on the behaviour of this man confronted with death: the supreme effort to survive, the increasing hopelessness of his position, and the futile attempt by the mind to preserve normality. One way of looking at the structure of the story is — like Yurkievich (*19*, p.222) and Shoemaker (*43*, p.250) — to divide it into 'cinco escenas y dos cuadros':

1. 'El hombre pisó algo blanduzco... un nuevo juramento.'
2. 'Llegó por fin al rancho... en la rueda de palo.'
3. 'Pero el hombre no quería morir... estaban disgustados.'
4. 'La corriente del río... a la deriva.'
CUADRO I: 'El Paraná corre allí... una majestad única.'
5. 'El sol había caído ya... Y cesó de respirar.'
CUADRO II: 'El cielo, al poniente...'

But this framework tends to stress the sequence of events — the external rather than the internal features of the story. For the purpose of studying Quiroga's treatment of dying, the overall development is better considered as consisting of two main phases, the first dominated by action and sensation, the second by inner thought and river scenery.

As the story begins there is no attention whatsoever to the protagonist's mind: it is all a question of movement and feeling. He treads on something, feels it to be soft, feels the bite, jumps ahead, turns, sees a snake in a defensive posture, and swears. Other actions follow swiftly during the first half of the story. After killing the snake and binding his wound, he returns home, where he calls his wife and drinks three glasses of rum. He then climbs into his canoe, paddles to the centre of the Paraná, moors the canoe beside Alves's land, drags himself twenty yards up the slope, calls for help, and finally returns to his canoe. Meanwhile Quiroga gives some attention to the wound itself: the two spots of blood that are quickly transformed into a huge swelling, which spreads from his leg into the lower part of his body. He also focuses on the acute pain, burning thirst and nausea — physical sensations that dominate this phase of the man's experience of dying, overriding his normal sensations (he can not taste the rum). In the third paragraph we read that the man 'durante un instante contempló'. It is a pause in his movements during which he presumably assesses his predicament, but Quiroga is still not ready to record his thoughts, for what he is emphasising is vitality and urgency, acute pain and the man's instinctive need for swift action to save himself. Hints of emotion then appear sporadically, although our cooperation is required for inferring the facts. We imagine a certain desperation as well as pain in the shouted conversation with his wife (an abrupt demand and a false recrimination, introduced by the author's hyperbolic terms 'en un estentor' and 'rugió'). In due course further succinct hints of the man's thought process follow: 'Bueno; esto se pone feo... murmuró entonces' (his self-control is gaining ascendancy, as he coolly assesses his predicament); 'Pero el hombre no quería morir' (he is hardening his resolve and rationalizing the instinct for self-preservation); 'con sombría energía' (determination, and a sense of the desperate nature of his plight); etc. A wealth of detail is suggested by succinct references of this kind, but he does not yet permit the thoughts to acquire any focus.

The end of this phase dominated by action and pain comes, naturally, with the man's last physical movements, when he reaches his canoe 'y la corriente, cogiéndola de nuevo, la llevó velozmente a la deriva' (p.62). From this point where his own capacity to act is exhausted, his fate is removed from his control, and he is at the mercy of natural processes: the chemical process of the poison, the current of the river. In this second phase there is a total absence of physical action on the part of the protagonist, a complete lack of description of the wound's visual appearance, and a great diminution in references to tactile experience. On the other hand the man's thoughts become dominant, and once all pain has dissipated the process of dying becomes converted into hopes and memories (at first rambling, but gradually more precise), which suggest the psychological need to maintain a grip on familiar reality and to hold a belief in the certainty of past and future.

Also, for the first time the landscape is described. There are two separate passages depicting the scenery, with similar though not identical functions. At their simplest level, both serve to give the story a credible setting in reality, for they mention place names ('el Paraná', 'la costa paraguaya') and local phenomena (the dark cliffs do literally border the river at that point, and macaws are among the birds of that region). But of course this does not explain Quiroga's emphasis on one or two specific aspects of each scene. In the first description of river scenery ('El Paraná corre allí en el fondo de una inmensa hoya... su belleza sombría y calma cobra una majestad única', p.62) the choice of vocabulary creates an unmistakable cumulative effect: 'fúnebremente', 'negros', 'negro', 'eterna', 'lúgubre', 'incesantes', 'fangosa', 'agresivo', 'silencio de muerte', 'sombría y calma'. These are words evoking not only darkness but associations with some threatening power and with death. The cliffs have an imposing effect ('encajonan' also brings to mind a coffin, of course), and the gigantic proportions of the rock dwarf the human being. Such a description forms an indelible imprint on our mind, leaving us in no doubt that the author is conveying a pictorial impression of a dying man's journey into death. When the sun has set and the man has shivered violently, we are already predisposed to see the fallacy of his apparent improvement, and his optimism does not seem justified.

The last sentence of the description changes the whole emphasis significantly, turning our attention to the beauty and majesty of the landscape. It is this aspect that Quiroga evokes at greater length in the second of the two descriptions, which begins with the words 'El cielo, al poniente, se abría ahora en pantalla de oro...' (p.62). The colours, the fragrance and the sight of wild life are reminders of the beauty of nature which the dying man is enjoying for the last time. Unlike the man, they are eternal. However, the process of dying is itself an endlessly repeated human experience: death itself is eternal, part of this natural process. In this way Quiroga augments the significance of the event he is relating, endowing death with an aura of grandeur and majesty, like the landscape.[15]

A last important ingredient in the treatment of death in 'A la deriva' is the symbolic value of the protagonist's canoe journey. Before any extravagant ideas are introduced it must be emphasized that the river provides people in that region with their chief means of transport. It is not merely, then, a literary symbol, but a local reality which reappears in other stories whose theme is not death. Quiroga was familiar with world literature, however, and knew that such writers as Aristophanes, Plato, Pausanias and Dante had referred to Lethe as a mythological river of the underworld whose waters were drunk by the dead to provide oblivion of the past. He also knew, therefore, that he had created an image of a dying man's journey out of this world. The role of the current should not be overlooked. Once the man is immobilized his body is at the mercy of this remorseless natural force which bears him in a single, inevitable direction. And a neat link with the idea of Time is made by the awareness that the rate of the current's flow will transport the dying man to assistance in five hours, whereas the rate of deterioration will carry him beyond recovery in two or three hours. Again, the current's flow is shown to hold power over the flow of life.

'La insolación'

Like 'A la deriva', 'La insolación' develops in such a way that a fatal outcome eventually seems inevitable. But in this story what Quiroga traces is not the process of dying but the course of events leading towards death; not the way a man copes with a

[15] R.H. Shoemaker convincingly refutes the view that these landscape descriptions serve to externalize the protagonist's frame of mind, though he concludes — less persuasively, it seems to me — that they emphasize nature's indifference to the death of a human being (*43*, p.254).

fatal situation but the way he brings one upon himself. For whereas the original agent of death in 'A la deriva' is unforeseen, in 'La insolación' it is wholly predictable. (This is also, incidentally, the story of five dogs whose lives are closely connected with that of their master — but that aspect of the tale belongs to Chapter 5.) A sense of inevitability is achieved by constant reminders of death's menace. On a cotton plantation in the Chaco, during the intense heat of early afternoon, five dogs see an apparition of their master, Jones; realizing that it is not him in person, they recognize the figure as a manifestation of Death. The following day they watch as míster Jones sends a labourer on horseback to the nearby timber yard to obtain a replacement for a broken bolt on his weeding machine. A little later they see an apparition of the horse enter the farmyard and collapse, and they recognize this as an omen of the horse's death. Indeed, almost immediately the labourer returns, having disregarded instructions not to gallop, and his horse falls dead with heat exhaustion. The conditions have been established: severe heat intensified by an exceptional drought. The dogs' two premonitions have presented unmistakable warnings. Although the dogs are temporarily satisfied that death has chosen a different victim, we have a sense of foreboding when — still without the bolt for his weeder — Jones sets out on foot to obtain it himself. The heat is further emphasized as the dogs reluctantly follow him, seeking every piece of shade on the way. Míster Jones has accomplished his mission and is within sight of his farm on the return journey when he feels overwhelmed with exhaustion. With his death now fully expected, its inevitability is illustrated by means of a graphic device. His dogs watch as Death in human form (an apparition of míster Jones) comes into sight walking towards the real man. Quiroga's master stroke is in the fact that the apparition walks in a direction that will lead, not to a head-on collision with Jones, but to an oblique encounter with him, provided that their respective speeds exactly coincide. Warning barks from the dogs prove futile, for their master is unable to perceive what is clear to the dogs: that his course and speed will bring him to an unavoidable encounter with Death. It is an effective way of stressing the supreme power of death and the helpless predicament of the human being.

While little attention is paid to the cause of Paulino's accident in 'A la deriva', considerable importance is attached to the circumstances producing míster Jones's sunstroke. Human fallibility is a major factor. In the face of difficult conditions Jones displays determination and effort, but his mistake is in losing a sense of prudence. Although he is tough ('resistía el sol como un peón') he has the same basic limitations as any human being or animal. Had he fully adapted to local conditions he would recognize the need to shelter from the sun when it is at its most severe. His indiscretion is compounded by an excessive consumption of whisky (alcohol is a predisposing factor in some cases of fatal sunstroke), and by the desire to walk off his anger towards the inefficient labourer. Finally, he commits the elementary error of taking a short cut instead of following the path, and this involves him in excessive expenditure of energy to cope with the difficult terrain. In other words, it is an essentially avoidable death which becomes inevitable.

Apart from two or three paragraphs, the whole narrative traces events from the standpoint of the dogs. Although their role is not merely a subsidiary one, it does have important advantages for a study of their master's fate. One element is the contrast between their behaviour and their master's. They are not indigenous animals but fox-terriers, with their origin — like that of míster Jones — in a remote land. Unlike their master, however, they allow themselves to be guided by natural instinct, which means that they shelter from the sun and avoid strenuous effort. By adapting to local conditions they form the harmonious relationship with nature that is essential for survival. Their other supporting role in the story is to make possible the supernatural previews of death. Quiroga has already broken out of the confines of literal reality by recording the thoughts, feelings and speech of dogs. From here it is only one step further to present their premonitions or sixth sense in visual form — a personification of death which endows it with an awesome menace and an eerie purposefulness. One critic even believes that the supernatural visions of death coming in advance suggest that 'El mundo está hecho de fuerzas amenazantes que no siempre podemos controlar — la Muerte, la Naturaleza en su colmo —' (*20*, p.136). This is a little too sweeping: the problem is human error when the natural menace is at its greatest. Nature, which in this story does not reflect moods, is both the agent of death and the geographical setting. Just as the remoteness of Misiones makes a fatal snake-bite possible in 'A la deriva', the heat in the Chaco during summer makes fatal sunstroke possible. Like the human condition itself, the natural environment is not essentially hostile to life, but overconfidence, inattentiveness or weakness can lead a person to annihilation in his prime.

'Nuestro primer cigarro'

In three stories where the protagonist himself does not die, fatalities have an important subsidiary function. The death of Lidia's mother in 'Una estación de amor', though not crucial to the plot, adds to the sombre mood in the winter of the love affair. 'Los buques suicidantes' depends for much of its tension upon the menace of death, which is greatly enhanced by the series of suicides. But the most interesting of the three is 'Nuestro primer cigarro'. Underneath the jocular surface of child's play runs a grim vein of adult anxiety and grief. Although the principal issue is a memorable formative episode in a child's process of growing up, one of the main aspects is the juvenile attitude towards death. The narrator, who is more interested in remembering the 'alegría' of those childhood days than the loss of an aunt, creates a paradoxical effect in his first sentence by implying that joy can derive from somebody's death. Quiroga emphasizes the lack of sympathy in order to stress the eight-year-old child's innocent awareness of death's terror. The incongruity caused by the clash of young innocence and the underlying sombre reality is again expressed linguistically in the sentence: 'Desde luego, a mi hermana y a mí nos entusiasmó el drama' (p.121). The fun of living in a different house, the pride in being the centre of attention, the opportunity to play games of adventure and discovery — these excitements remove Lucía's smallpox to the background. Although they are aware of the danger that they might have been infected, the children are not preoccupied. All the danger belongs to another world, from which only occasional signs reach them: 'fuerte agitación', 'puertas que se abrían', 'semblantes asustados' (p.121), so that when Lucía's death occurs it merits only an indirect mention as a cause of their heroic exile.

This unconcern about death is integral to the trick later played on Uncle Alfonso. In its first version the title of this story, 'El cigarro pateador', drew undue attention to the less significant of the jokes: the firework disguised as a cigar, dangerous and thoughtless, but too playful to be taken as a serious threat of fatality. But the new title emphasizes the main episode, in which revenge on Uncle Alfonso and uncomfortable initiation coincide. The boy's first instinct is to escape from his irate uncle and to hide. But when he realizes that the sound of a rock splashing into the bottom of a well could be mistaken for his own body, he is delighted at the implications. The victorious aspects of this situation are clear: Uncle Alfonso's anxiety and disgrace, leading to a greater respect for Eduardo; the boy's heroic initiation into smoking, which proves a perfect strategy to save him from difficult explanations. There is another aspect, however, in which the whole experience becomes a partial destruction of innocence, and in this aspect the tables are turned. It is not the fact that his presumed death hurts his mother, for her grief barely filters through the narrative, and Eduardo is comforted by the pleasure that his reappearance will give. It is what he discovers — from his privileged and unusual vantage point — about the attitude of other people to his demise. Only his mother shows affliction on his account; the other people are more preoccupied with her feelings than with the fact that he is missing, presumed dead. In effect, his supposed death causes no greater sorrow among others (with the exception of his mother) than his aunt's death had caused in him. Without making the point explicitly, Quiroga was indicating Ernesto's rueful lesson that one person's death barely impinges on the world at large.

It is evident from the stories examined in this and the previous chapter that Quiroga greatly varied his handling of death. It can be predictable ('La insolación') or unexpected ('El solitario'), the result of error ('La miel silvestre') or of something beyond human control ('El almohadón de plumas'), pitiable ('Una estación de amor'), gruesome ('La gallina degollada'), noble ('A la deriva'), or even a source of indifference ('Nuestro primer cigarro'). But there is an overall tendency for him to depict situations in which death is foreseeable, avoidable, the clear result of human error, and inspiring fear, pity and horror. In a letter written during the last year of his life, Quiroga explained that when he was younger death was for him a source of fear: 'Estaba al punto de temer exclusivamente a la muerte, si prematura' (*15*, p.107). An early death, he felt, would have prevented him from fulfilling his potential to create. Now that he felt that he had completed his work, however, he could write: 'No temo a la muerte, amigo, porque ella significa descanso.' Later that same year he acknowledged that he now saw death as a natural process by means of which he would respond to the laws of nature: 'He de morir regando mis plantas, y plantando el mismo día de morir. No hago más que integrarme en la naturaleza, con sus leyes y armonías oscurísimas aún para nosotros, pero existentes' (*15*, p.113).[16] It was certainly a far cry from the view he had held at the time of *Cuentos de amor de locura y de muerte*.

---

[16] This attitude forms the basis of the story 'Las moscas' (1933) in *Más allá*.

5. The Bush

Features of the local setting

When he assessed his career in 1936 Quiroga emphasized that the man of action in him — the 'pioneer agrícola' — was as important as the writer (*12*, I, p.72). Although his opinion should not be taken too literally, the pride in his achievements in the *monte* (or bush country) led him to attach especial importance to his stories about the lives of pioneers in that region. Six of the *Cuentos de amor de locura y de muerte* depend substantially on their setting in Misiones: 'A la deriva', 'El alambre de púa', 'Los mensú', 'Yaguaí', 'Los pescadores de vigas', and 'La miel silvestre'. A seventh story, 'La insolación', which is set in the Chaco, has similar characteristics and will be mentioned from time to time in this chapter.

During the years when he was writing stories like 'El alambre de púa' and 'Yaguaí' Quiroga was also dispatching to *Caras y Caretas* and *Fray Mocho* a series of articles describing features of life in the *monte*. In 1912 he published 'El arte de cazar en los bosques de Misiones', 'Las hormigas carnívoras', and 'El oro vegetal' (which is about *yerba mate*); in 1913 'Seda y vino de naranja', 'Los vencedores' (about healers of snake bites), and 'Las víboras venenosas del Norte'. Further articles on ants, cassava, sugar and many other topics were to follow. This eagerness to share his local knowledge with novices in the distant city of Buenos Aires underlies remarks occasionally slipped into his short stories for emphasis, such as the parenthesis '— y es preciso saber lo que esto supone en Misiones —' ('Yaguaí', p.105). It is a slightly condescending viewpoint which from time to time served to remind readers of the realities on which these fictitious tales were based.

One of the principal influences that this attitude exerted on his fiction was the inclusion of numerous features of the local

setting. 'El alambre de púa' offers a good example. The two
horses belong to a *chacra* (a smallholding) where their paddock
is surrounded by a hedge of *capuera*, which — Quiroga helpfully
informs us — is impenetrably thick new growth from felled
trees. Their escape route through a grove of *chirca* trees leads
them across a narrow strip of sparse woodland, into a patch of
capuera topped by wild tobacco plants. The wildness of the area
has been tempered by tracts of land with wire fencing: banana
and *yerba mate* plantations, a field of oats, and pastures where
cattle graze. 'Yaguaí' also takes place in a region of small-
holdings, where bananas, beans, maize and cassava are grown
and hens are kept, and in mentioning the rivers Paraná and
Yabebirí Quiroga almost pinpoints the geographic location. In
addition to plants and animals found almost anywhere he introduces into 'Yaguaí' a number of the more local varieties (some
of the names being derived from the local Guaraní language):
the *catiguá* tree, the *irara* ferret, the racoon-like *coatí*, an
armadillo known in the region as the *tateto*, and a similar
creature called the *tatú*, rodents such as the *apereá* and *agutí*,
and two birds in the partridge family: the *urú* and the *martineta*.
By and large it would be inaccurate, however, to claim that this
regional material is presented merely as information interesting
in its own right, in the manner of *costumbrista* fiction of the
nineteenth century. As we shall notice shortly, the purpose is to
create a vivid impression of a real setting in which the juxta-
position of human civilization and nature creates dramatic
tension. Directly from this springs the stories' action.

Extreme conditions

One or two aspects of the topography and climate play a predominant role. Not surprisingly, of the few place names to
appear it is not those of the towns and villages that stand out
(Tacurú-Pucú, Posadas, San Ignacio, and Puerto Felicidad) but
those of the River Paraná and its tributaries (such as the distant
Iguazú, and the closer Guayra, Teyucuaré, Ñacanguazú,
Paranaí and Yabebirí). For not only do they serve as a point of
reference but the region's whole way of life is to a large extent

controlled by them.

The Paraná figures prominently in four of the stories under discussion. Its dominance is perhaps greatest in 'A la deriva' where, as we observed in Chapter 4, far more than a background it is one of the participants in the action, holding the man's life in its current, reflecting first an atmosphere of funereal gloom and later an air of majestic beauty, acting as the representative of permanent nature, perhaps to contrast with human transitoriness and perhaps, also, to suggest that a human death is itself no more than a part of nature. In 'Yaguaí', where the effects of drought are being demonstrated, and the Paraná has its strength diminished, it is still treated with the respect one reserves for a sleeping beast: 'El Paraná yacía, muerto a esa hora en su agua de cine, esperando la caída de la tarde para revivir' (p.99). In two other stories Quiroga demonstrates the power of the river in flood. The unfortunate Cayé and Podeley ('Los mensú'), who hope to use the Paraná as their transport to freedom, encounter it at its most hostile: cold, swollen, twisting and rocking their raft until it begins to sink. It is described as 'el río salvaje', and its imprisoning and menacing aspect is indicated in terms closely similar to those in 'A la deriva': 'encajonado en los lúgubres murallones del bosque' (p.93). Not merely the scene of Podeley's death, it is actually inimical to the man's feverish condition. Cayé too, who sits for days 'con los ojos fijos en el Paraná', realises that the river is his one hope of salvation — which indeed it proves to be. 'Los pescadores de vigas' offers another instance of the Paraná in flood and at its most severe. Although strictly the pretext for testing Candiyú's valour, strength, determination and skill, the river acquires features converting it into a formidable adversary, its weapons being the current, snakes, and uprooted trees, its victims being the dead animals and the human corpse. Candiyú's success represents a human triumph, though the narrative glances ahead to the same man later, sick and bed-ridden, living on the shores of the Paraná which (Quiroga does not need to remind us) remains unchanged. Overall, however, it is not regarded as something malignant. Dominant and majestic, it inspires awe, respect, and sometimes admiration, and it serves Quiroga as one of nature's principal agents in his study of human civilization in relation to the environment.

There is a tendency for Quiroga to show the climate of Misiones in unusual or even extreme conditions. For fifty-two consecutive hours the rain beats down in 'Los pescadores de vigas'. It pauses for two hours, the air heavy with moisture, and then the deluge recommences. Under these conditions the lumberjacks must work. Quiroga stresses the discomfort and difficulty caused when human activity is dependent on natural conditions: 'y mientras el temporal siguió, los peones continuaron gritando, cayéndose y tumbando bajo el agua helada' (p.112). Similarly, in 'Los mensú' it is the onset of wet weather and the need for the labourers to continue working exposed to the elements that combine to cause a recurrence of Podeley's malaria and to precipitate his escape from the lumber camp. The climate thereby becomes the clearest manifestation of adverse forces operating against the labourers.

If it is not prolonged heavy rain it is abnormally high temperatures and exceptionally severe droughts that enhance natural problems in Quiroga's stories. The Chaco's sun plays a major role in 'La insolación', affecting animals and humans from the moment it rises, and claiming the lives of the horse and míster Jones when it is near its zenith. Conditions are exacerbated by the dry spell, which has caused temperatures to increase for three consecutive days. In 'Yaguaí' an even greater emphasis is given to the extreme circumstances. From the third sentence Quiroga draws attention to the 'sol a mediodía de Misiones', the hot north wind, the thermometer at 40° centigrade, the 'mediodía de fuego', and the 'calor tropical' in which Yaguaí has successfully proved some degree of adaptability and ingenuity. With the wind obstinately blowing from the north, however, the dry spell becomes a drought whose effects are described at length by references to the thermometer, the shrivelling of the crops, and the new behaviour of the wild life. Yaguaí's own conduct is assessed by his ability to withstand the adverse conditions. In fact, it is the drought that directly causes his change of fortune and is indirectly responsible for his death. For it is only because of the hard times that Cooper lends the dog to Fragoso; it is the scarcity of food that compels Yaguaí to acquire 'el aspecto humillado, servil y traicionero de los perros del país'; and it is the increased marauding of such neighbouring dogs that gives Cooper an itching trigger finger.

Other dangers that exist naturally in the bush may be added to the threat of floods, sunstroke and drought. In 'A la deriva' it is a venomous snake, and in 'La miel silvestre' it is carnivorous ants. The impression that emerges tends, therefore, to emphasize the inhospitable and hostile aspects of the area. Quiroga would have admitted that this was an exaggeration of the reality. In an article submitted to the Buenos Aires daily newspaper *La Nación* entitled 'Misiones' he stressed the fact that where human beings have cleared the bush and are regularly present the wild creatures timorously keep their distance. The pioneer's only constant enemy is the forest, which threatens to take control again if he is inattentive. Moreover, although drought, high temperatures, heavy rainfall and even frosts can occur, Quiroga actually claimed that the weather is on the whole one of the region's attractive features: 'Fuera de estos límites extremos que hemos acentuado ex profeso, el clima de Misiones constituye todo él un aura de dulzura y vitalidad' (*14*, p.99). In other words, when composing the short stories he intensified the natural conditions in order to create crises. In the face of these conditions his protagonists reveal their true worth and — frequently — meet their death.

Man and the wilds

In the same article, 'Misiones', the pioneer's life is described as 'la lucha feroz contra la soledad, la planta, el animal — el desamparo en su más áspera desnudez — que debe librar el poblador de vanguardia para sostenerse en pie...' (*14*, p.101). Quiroga's fictional characters confirm this impression. Paulino's remoteness from civilization ('A la deriva') and míster Jones's 'solitaria velada de *whisky*' each night ('La insolación') directly contribute to their fate. Ramírez is involved in a constant struggle to defend his crop of oats against the bull and the cows ('El alambre de púa'), and his banana plantation has been burned by the frost. Cooper and his family of two children (reminiscent of Quiroga's own family) endure hard times with the drought, which causes deer to eat his beans and dogs to plunder his hens ('Yaguaí'). The loss of the children's pet, Yaguaí, exacerbates their misfortune. Even more detrimental are the drought's effects on Fragoso's smallholding. His maize and beans have been killed by lack of moisture, and an invasion of rats destroys his new crop of maize.

A few of Quiroga's pioneering characters are owners and employees of timber and *yerba mate* companies, like the accountant míster Hall, the foreman Fernández, and the owner Castelhum in 'Los pescadores de vigas', whose circumstances do not appear to be particularly arduous. But Quiroga is far more interested in the labourers, both on the farms and in the lumber camps. In Chapter 6 the social issues raised by such handling will be considered, but it is important for us to note here that Quiroga depicts them sharing the same tough conditions to which his settlers are subjected. Esteban Podeley and Cayetano Maidana of 'Los mensú' and Candiyú and other *peones* of 'Los pescadores de vigas' face torrential rain and swollen rivers, while the *peones* in 'Yaguaí' and 'La insolación' are briefly mentioned during the droughts that afflict Misiones and the Chaco. The underlying purpose in these stories, however, is to demonstrate the achievements of the characters rather than their misery. As Quiroga once remarked, 'la vida, aun en Misiones, no vale sino cuando hay que conquistarla duramente' (*14*, p.100).

All this forms part of a more general theme of human civilization in relation to the world of nature. It is a theme charged with complexity and paradox, where the author's attitude to the settler quietly adjusting to his new environment contrasts with his treatment of the city man theatening to alter the balance of nature, and where the point of view adopted by the narrative is not always that of mankind but sometimes that of the animal world.

'La miel silvestre' illustrates what Quiroga regarded as one of the worst aspects of people's contact with the wild regions. It is a tale of a city man inexperienced in Misiones and lacking the necessary prudence and caution to survive. The accountant is given an ironical surname — Benincasa — to emphasize his incongruity in the countryside. His attitude to visiting the region lacks due seriousness ('Quiso honrar su vida aceitada con dos o tres choques de vida intensa' — childish search for easy adventure), and he is both temperamentally unsuitable and thoroughly immersed in city habits. In Chapter 1 we saw how Quiroga's own first visit to Misiones was that of a hot-headed and ill-equipped novice. So scornful was he of his own mistakes that he returned to the subject again in a strikingly similar story, 'Los Robinsones del bosque' (1916), which ends with a clear message that the wilderness must be treated with caution and common sense: 'El bosque es hostil exclusivamente a dos clases de personas: las que no creen en las víboras, y las que las ven a cada paso...' (*14*, p.68).

A constant source of tension between man and nature is the destruction of the forest, the animals' natural habitat, by machetes and fire. Although our collection does not raise this problem directly we should keep in mind the prominence given to it in stories elsewhere such as 'Anaconda', where the snake population believe that 'Hombre y Devastación son sinónimos' (*3*, p.8). In the absence of any simple solution, a struggle will inevitably continue between humans and animals. Quiroga appeared to regard such a struggle as acceptable provided the balance is not altered excessively in favour of human civilization. He recognized that a struggle for survival is inherent in the natural state of affairs in the bush. The extreme conditions depicted in 'Yaguaí' show that hunting, at first no more than a sport, can become an indispensable activity. Cooper and a farm worker need to hunt deer that are attacking their beans; Fragoso hunts the rats that infest his maize; Yaguaí and other dogs seek their own food, sometimes seizing a hen; in fact all creatures — wild animals, domesticated animals and human beings — are shown in 'Yaguaí' to need to hunt for their survival. Outside our collection again, Quiroga's narrator in the story 'La patria' explains that in the forest, despite the struggles and the bloodshed, there is a constant liberty, and when all the species are free 'en la selva ensangrentada reina la paz' (*4*, p.108). The animals in 'La patria' accept a human settler in their midst on the grounds that 'Si está aquí en la selva, es libre. El nos puede matar, y nosotros podemos también matarlo a él' (*4*, p.109). In 'La miel silvestre' Quiroga shows at the expense of the unfortunate Benincasa that no creature may reserve the right to be hunter.

The primeval urge to hunt was for Quiroga 'el lazo más prolongado, persistente y tenaz que une al hombre con-temporáneo con su pasado ancestral...' (*14*, pp.82-83). His own fondness for hunting led him to cater for readers — like children — who prefer a simplified view of man's relationship with nature, highlighted by danger and adventure, as in the ten stories published in the magazine *Billiken* under the general heading 'El hombre frente a las fieras' (1924). (The Editors warn their readers that 'Varias de estas cartas están manchadas con sangre'.) This is not the treatment found in *Cuentos de amor de locura y de muerte* and most other collections, for Quiroga recognized the paradoxical aspects of the hunter's attitude towards animals. He once recalled the re-awakening of his hunting instinct back in Misiones after a period of ten years in the city when, hearing the sound of dogs that had cornered an animal in the forest nearby, he seized a machete and joined them. Some months later his children's pet deer had strayed and been shot. Presuming that the hunter was a boy with a pistol, Quiroga remembered the numerous creatures that he too had killed. 'Aprecié por primera vez lo que es apropiarse de una existencia. Y comprendí el valor de una vida ajena...' (*14*, p.87).

The animal point of view

In the light of these comments on hunting it is clear that Quiroga did not consider a human life to be different in essence from an animal life, or the human point of view to be the only one worth adopting in the relationship between the species. The dog rather than its owners is the protagonist of 'Yaguaí', and the events are traced mainly from his standpoint. We admire Yaguaí's adaptability and ingenuity, we are amused by his antics, and above all we sympathize with his predicament, wonder how he will cope with it, and grieve over his death. 'La insolación' is another case: although the focus switches from the dogs to their owner during the last pages, the tale ends appropriately with a comment on the change of fortune that befalls them as a result of míster Jones's death. It is not a story quite like 'Yaguaí' with the spotlight obviously directed at the animals rather than the humans, but it does demonstrate the general point that Quiroga found both sides worthy of attention and sympathy.

The most interesting example is 'El alambre de púa', a story narrated entirely from the point of view of animals, exposing a difference of attitude among them, and tracing a struggle between them and humans. Seen as a whole, this is a tale of the impact of human settlers on nature. It covers the theme of the natural yearning for liberty, and traces various aspects of co-existence between the species. Significantly, Quiroga has chosen as his standpoint that of two semi-domesticated animals. Through these horses he illustrates, in the first phase of the story, the instinct of all creatures to seek their freedom. After discovering a gap in the thick barrier of undergrowth that surrounds their paddock, the horses wander at will through the countryside. Two other fences offer no serious problem to them, for they simply search patiently until a breach is discovered. Human efforts to exert a physical control over the movement of animals in this area are therefore partially counteracted by the natural processes whereby trees rot and collapse, breaking the barriers. In this attempt of man to exert his domination there is no complete victory, only a constant struggle in which he and nature find a kind of equilibrium. The horses, it will be noticed, do not attempt to make a permanent escape, but return to their farm at evening for their food. As a symbol of their dependence both wear a rope around the neck. The cattle, however, 'atrevidas y astutas, impenitentes invasoras de chacras y del Código Rural' (pp.75-76), are naturally rebellious and show no respect for a code of behaviour imposed by mankind. They represent more strongly nature's resistance to the territorial claims made by humans.

What brings matters to a head is the development of this tension between man and cattle into a private contest between

the smallholder Ramírez and the bull Barigüí. Although the use
of barbed wire proves sufficient to keep horses and cows from
invading the crop of oats, it is in itself an inadequate measure
against the determination and power of the bull. Ramírez,
however, employs his intelligence to good effect: he can not keep
Barigüí out of his field, but he can make the barbed wire fence
so taut that when the bull, challenged, uses brute force to beat a
hasty retreat his skin is badly lacerated and he will never repeat
the invasion. Barigüí's final ignominy at the hands of human
beings occurs when his owner, Zaninski, decides to have him
slaughtered rather than incur the expense of a possibly fruitless
effort to cure his injuries. It is an emphatic way of making the
point that in individual instances human intelligence will
inevitably triumph against nature's blind strength. For their survival, animals might adopt the more circumspect behaviour of
the horses — an idea underlined at the end by the irony of one of
the horses carrying meat from the slaughtered bull to the
owner's house.

It is important for us to bear in mind that this is not the story
of virgin nature's reaction to the arrival of human beings in the
district. Ramírez's fences and crops, Zaninski's cattle, the
horses and their farm, have all become integrated in the local
countryside. What 'El alambre de púa' illustrates is Quiroga's
reaction to a slow and continuous process in which man and
animals learn to coexist. He is showing here not the impact of
human civilization as a relentless, destructive force (as he
occasionally does in other collections), but the impact of settlers
who, like the animals, seek to live off the land. It is a natural
aspect of this coexistence that there should be disputes over territory, plunder and defence. The humans' superior intellect
inevitably promises them a degree of domination, but Quiroga
reminds us that this will never be complete. He appears to
acknowledge the right of Ramírez to use a fence to exclude
animals but equally recognizes the instinct of animals to escape
through fences that imprison them. This same instinct can lead
them into dangerous situations. When they penetrate a fence in
order to eat a settler's crop, animals are acting quite naturally
but, of course, they suffer the natural consequences.

Another feature of 'El alambre de púa' and 'La insolación' is that the animal characters are endowed with the power of speech. Although this is a time-honoured literary practice, it was probably Rudyard Kipling who most directly inspired Quiroga, with stories like those in *The Jungle Book* (1894). In the Uruguayan's own *Cuentos de la selva (para niños)* (1918) half of the tales even allow the animals to converse with human beings, in the way that Kipling's Mowgli converses with wolves and a tiger. In his other collections, however, this is rare.[17] It is evident that in 'El alambre de púa' and 'La insolación' he approached the matter of talking animals with caution. Before a word is spoken, the narrative in each story clearly establishes the fact that events and sensations are all being perceived by the senses of animals. When the first thoughts are expressed aloud they are bald statements representing no more than simple, basic reactions, as though the intention were not to exceed the capacity of a sub-human intelligence:

— Un alambrado — dijo el alazán.
—Sí, un alambrado — asintió el malacara.
('El alambre de púa', p.73)

Old, que miraba hacía rato la vera del monte, observó:
—La mañana es fresca.
Milk siguió la mirada del cachorro y quedó con la vista fija, parpadeando distraído. Después de un rato, dijo:
— En aquel árbol hay dos halcones.
('La insolación', p.64)

These limits are quite deliberately maintained throughout both stories. At times Quiroga's efforts to suggest the animals' inability to rationalize become conspicuous. For example, the horses are dimly aware that some kind of special problem is posed by Ramírez's latest barbed wire fence, but they can only gaze at it, thinking 'confusamente'. One of them tenaciously applies his mind to the issue: '— Los hilos están muy estirados...

[17] 'El canto del cisne' (*Anaconda*), 'La patria' (*El desierto*), 'Juan Darién' (*El desierto*), 'El potro salvaje' (*El desierto*), 'La señorita leona' (*Más allá*).

— observó aún el malacara, tratando siempre de precisar lo que sucedería si...' (p.82). His inability to complete the thought before the event takes place is represented by the suspension points. In 'La insolación' the words spoken aloud by the dogs amount to no more than sixteen utterances of half a line and two of a line. They all express the dogs' sensations, sights, and premonitions of death. In 'El alambre de púa' the total number of lines of dialogue spoken is substantially greater, but the principle of brevity and simplicity is the same. The animals' conversation is on a narrow range of topics: what they see, whether fences can retain them, whether the bull is more courageous than the horses, and whether a man can keep the bull out of his field. By this means the extent of fantasy in these two stories is limited, so that it is still possible for us to see them as ultimately realistic situations.

On the other hand, Quiroga clearly retained a slight interest in individualizing the personality of some of the animals. The young dog *Old* stands out from the other four by virtue of his liveliness, inexperience and curiosity. One important feature of 'La insolación' therefore becomes *Old*'s first encounter with death, and the reader is thus shown how universally death is feared. More attention is given to individual traits among the animals of 'El alambre de púa'. The two horses are distinguished by physical appearance — one a sorrel, the other with a white forehead — as well as by age and experience. Their docile nature is contrasted with the scornful haughtiness of the cows and the aggressive independence of the bull, whose name individualizes him more strongly than the others. (Barigüí, incidentally, was the name of one of Quiroga's own fox-terriers.) In the interrelation of horses, cows and bull there is of course a simplistic formulation of certain human attitudes. With the female observers impressed only by virile conduct, the two horses begin to see their escape as a relatively feeble action, and Barigüí's prowess against a human adversary becomes a display of *machismo*. Like other writers, Quiroga did occasionally use animal protagonists to voice human ideas and to comment on human behaviour. ('La abeja haragana', in *Cuentos de la selva*, obviously teaches young readers the dangers of laziness and the virtue of effort on behalf of the community.) But this does not appear to be his intention in any of the *Cuentos de amor de locura y de muerte*. The human attitudes recognizable among the animals of 'El alambre de púa' are an attempt to represent in a form that will be understood by humans the different instincts of different types of animal. In general, the effect is to convert animals into characters with whom the reader may more readily sympathize.

We have noticed, then, that in three stories the animals' standpoint is adopted, that in all three some attention is given to converting animals into individualized characters, and that in two of the tales the animals' communication with each other is represented as spoken words. In 'La insolación' there is a special purpose in endowing the dogs with the power of speech: that of creating a framework within which premonitions of death may be represented in dramatized form without provoking the reader's disbelief. But the overall purpose in these animal stories is to emphasize that man does not possess inherently superior rights. He must share in 'los sagrados derechos a la vida, de todos los seres del universo' (*4*, p.138).

6. Social Themes

In 1911 Quiroga declared himself a strong supporter of Uruguay's Colorado party on the grounds of its 'laicismo, obrerismo, progreso, y democracia íntima' (*12*, II, p.141). At that point in time José Batlle y Ordóñez, a Colorado who had served as president from 1903 to 1907, was about to begin his second term in office. The era dominated by his politics, which endured until 1929, saw the unification of Uruguay, the establishment of a role for the opposition party (the Blancos) within government, the introduction of economic nationalism, and the adoption of advanced social welfare measures. Although Quiroga had virtually no active involvement with the Colorado party, he was a personal friend of Baltasar Brum (who became president in 1917), and held Uruguayan consulate posts (which, incidentally, he treated as sinecures). Further evidence of his political position may be noticed in his attitude to the Buenos Aires strikes of 1919. His letters clearly indicate approval of mass movements leading to radical social change (*12*, II, p.66), and a readiness to take up his tools to cultivate the land again. However, in practice his position was less radical than this suggests. As a smallholder he had occasionally employed local casual labour, and his relations with the *peones* had not always been smooth. Mishandling of labour relations played no small part in the collapse of his enterprise as a cotton grower in the Chaco. Later, in Misiones, he encountered objections to the fact that he personally took part in the manual labour on his land. Deeply resenting this intrusion by the *peones* into his rights he complained: 'Han convertido el trabajo manual en casta aristocrática que quiere apoderarse del gran negocio del Estado' (*15*, pp.74-75). In perspective, therefore, Quiroga emerges as a person sympathetic to the proletariat in principle, and conscious of the need for greater social justice, but wary of any collective threat to the rights of the individual.

This moderately reformist, philanthropic outlook underlies the half-dozen stories on social themes distributed through his collections. One of them is included in *Cuentos de amor de locura y de muerte*.

In 1902 the Argentinian government began to investigate reports of atrocities committed in the timberyards of Misiones. Quiroga's story 'Los mensú' illustrates some of the social evils that were being perpetrated.[18] The core of the problem was the timber companies' exploitation of impecunious workers by means of debt slavery. In 'Los mensú' we follow two workers through the process of signing the contract, receiving advance wages, spending the money, travelling north up the River Paraná to the remote timberyard, and working off the debt. It becomes clear that one of the author's aims is to censure the extent of power that a company exerted over its employees. In order to bring the issue to a head he creates a situation in which one of the labourers falls ill (with malaria) and is in urgent need of professional medical attention down river. Quiroga manifestly invites the reader's strong disapproval of the foreman's refusal to concede leave of absence. Podeley has a reputation for reliability, he promises to return when cured, his account has only a relatively small sum outstanding, and above all the foreman displays a callous disregard for Podeley's life (he knows recovery is impossible at the timberyard, but 'prefería hombre muerto a deudor lejano', p.91). The author demonstrates that he supports Podeley's feeling of being unjustly treated and sees the logic of his decision to escape: 'Esta injusticia para con él creó lógica y velozmente el deseo del desquite' (p.91). His indictment of the system continues when armed men attempt to kill the fleeing labourers, and of course when Podeley meets his death because the timber company has driven him to such an extreme physical plight. To these points might be added the argument that throughout the story attention is focused on the *mensú*, and interest aroused in his way of life. Quiroga shows, for example, what Podeley's typical working day consists of: long hours, dull food and hard labour, with his

[18] The term *mensú* (from *mensual*) was used locally to refer to *peones* employed for a fixed number of months in lumber camps, *yerba mate* plantations, etc.

body exposed to insects. It is a routine compounded by days of tedium sheltering from the rain and offset only by a visit to the store on Sundays. Even in the store there are rising prices to endure.

Quiroga's point of view, however, is not that of a crude apologist. Besides inviting our disapproval of the company's harsh and unjust conduct, he also invites our consideration of the reasons why the *mensú* continued to sign the contracts that bound him to this miserable existence. The political campaigner might well have drawn attention to the labourer's impoverished and uneducated background, the lack of alternative employment, or the hardships of a dependent family. But significantly none of this occupies any attention. What Quiroga appears to treat as the cause is an innate foible in the *mensú*. This is what he implies (without actually using the negative term) when he informs us that although ninety-eight per cent of *peones* are without money when they arrive in Posadas, their wish to spend a few days living in expensive merriment overrides other considerations: 'Un instante después estaban borrachos y con nueva contrata firmada. ¿En qué trabajo? ¿En dónde? No lo sabían, ni les importaba tampoco' (p.84). These words convey all the disproportion of such behaviour. The lack of resistance, the loss of self-control, and the absence of due concern are compressed into a matter of three or four lines, while a page or more is then devoted to an account of their good time. After admiring Cayé for his determination and endurance in making a successful escape from the timberyard, Quiroga closes the story with renewed and enhanced emphasis on the *mensú*'s inability to escape from the imprisoning condition of his habits. The author's intentions are exaggerated by the technique of deliberate juxtapositioning on the final page. Cayé fears for his life, arrives safely in Posadas, and commits himself to a new contract within the space of six lines. At this stage the author avoids the individualizing Christian name and makes use of the generic term 'el *mensú*' as a final reminder of the general predicament of men like him.

In perspective, then, it will be noticed that this story expresses compassion for labourers who were subject to debt slavery without propounding an outright condemnation of the system itself. It severely censures the companies' harsh treatment of employees, but it places some of the blame for the system on the men's eagerness to squander months of advance pay on days of pleasure. The social criticism is directed, in fact, at both sides of the system — employer and employee — and the story must be seen primarily not as a piece of propaganda but as the investigation and exposure of a way of life.

The theme of the *mensú* was again taken up by Quiroga in a film script, *La jangada* (unpublished during his lifetime), where a government inspector disguised as a labourer works in a timberyard to verify stories of injustice and degradation. The employer's treatment of his work force is even more callous than that in the short story. Moreover, Quiroga's directions indicate his own point of view more clearly: 'Orgaz [the inspector] constata la miseria del trabajo a que se somete a los peones, sin la menor garantía de salud, ni la más remota idea de volver un poco confortable la vida de gentes entregadas de cuerpo y alma al patrón'.[19] However Orgaz (a hero in the vein of Douglas Fairbanks Jr) follows a middle course between the employer and the *mensú*. When there is a violent uprising he saves the life of the ringleader (named Cayé) but hands him over to the law. Quiroga's directions here are extremely revealing: 'Diálogos de efecto aquí, pues él dará la piedra final de toque para apreciar y hacer más simpática la figura de Orgaz, a efectos del público *conservador*' (p.30; Quiroga's emphasis). In other words, having exposed the social injustice at length he is at pains not to alienate the sympathy of conservative cinema audiences. The solution to the labourers' problem offered in this film script is neither socialist nor anti-capitalist. Orgaz himself will become the new employer (married to the old employer's daughter) — the answer lies, that is to say, in enlightened management.

In *Cuentos de amor de locura y de muerte* no other story gives such prominence to a social theme, although many allow us to perceive the author's opinion of the society that he was depicting. 'Los pescadores de vigas', for example, offers a

[19] *Guión cinematográfico de 'La jangada'* (D.11, Archivo Horacio Quiroga, Instituto Nacional de Investigaciones y Archivos Literarios, Montevideo), p.12.

glimpse of life in the timberyards which complements the impression in 'Los mensú'. Castelhum's labourers, with an urgent task required of them, are being asked to work in appalling weather. Although Quiroga mentions briefly that their wages have been steeply increased, he spares two paragraphs to concentrate on their strenuous and united effort, their drenched clothes and thin bodies, and the dangers of slipping, being struck by logs, and falling ill with fever. On the other hand a less favourable picture of the *peones* is offered in 'La insolación'. Míster Jones's labourer disobeys his orders by galloping the horse and lacks the sense to realize that he is killing the animal in that intense heat. Quiroga implicitly shares míster Jones's exasperation with the man's apologies — 'sus jesuíticas disculpas'. To cap it all, the *peón* has failed to obtain the bolt for which he was sent, and again the author's impatience is perceptible in the unfinished sentence which explains his reasons: 'No había tornillo: el almacén estaba cerrado, el encargado dormía, etc.' (p.69).

For a comprehensive view of Quiroga's social themes we may add the oblique portrayal of bourgeois society found in the love stories, and noted in Chapter 2. The concern that a prospective partner's family should belong to the right social class helps to destroy relationships in two stories, permitting us to infer confidently that Quiroga regarded an excessive preoccupation with the matter to be a social fault. There is a degree of ambivalence in 'La meningitis y su sombra' where the narrator appears mildly scornful that María Elvira's family should worry about his background, while at the same time he barely disguises his pride at being of sufficient standing. There is no ambiguity, however, about the author's antipathy for Lidia's mother in 'Una estación de amor'. For her, the acquisition of money and the ambition to improve her daughter's status lead to dubious moral behaviour, which is condemned by the author as 'la moral[20] de las burguesas histéricas' (p.15). He finds equally worthy of censure the hypocrisy in middle-class society, a pretence of moral rectitude, the imposition upon other people of standards which the plaintiff himself has failed to uphold. In this respect the author

[20] The 17th edition erroneously reads 'lo mortal'.

agrees with the complaint made by Lidia's mother that Nébel's father is guilty of double standards.

Although one or two other social problems arise casually from time to time (for example, the lack of cooperation by the Polish settler Zaninski in 'El alambre de púa' and the quarrel of Paulino and his neighbour in 'A la deriva', which hint at a potential theme of difficult relations among the pioneers), none acquires sufficient prominence to warrant further consideration here. On the whole Quiroga did not use the short story as a vehicle for social or political comment. In reflecting the reality that he knew in Buenos Aires and Misiones he did not disguise his personal attitudes, but only occasionally did a social problem become a principal theme. Even in 'Los mensú', as we have seen, the impetus towards social reform is weakened by the author's attitude to the deeply-rooted habits of the labourers. Such stories may be classified as social realism, but not as social protest literature.

7. Structure, Point of View and Narrative Style

Structure

As a contributor to *Caras y Caretas*, Quiroga was subject to the severe discipline of the chief editor, Luis Pardo, who demanded that all short stories should be confined to 1256 words, or a single page including an illustration (*18*, p.95). Critics have tended to draw exaggerated conclusions from this information. The truth is that in *Cuentos de amor de locura y de muerte* only two stories are as short as this: 'Los buques suicidantes' and 'A la deriva'. Seven occupy the equivalent of one-and-a-half to two pages, four stories are about three of *Caras y Caretas*'s pages, and two — the first and the last — are substantially longer. Quiroga found a tight control good discipline for a new writer; in his later stories he expanded a little. Despite these words of caution, however, the emphatic point remains that brevity was always one of his main criteria. Even in 1928 he found 3,500 words 'más que suficiente' (*18*, p.94), and all but two in our collection meet that requirement.

One of the reasons for being brief, he argued, was the need to avoid losing the reader's interest. Closely allied to this was the artistic merit derived from intensity and energy. While a novel represented analysis, a short story should aim at synthesis. The writer of stories should go straight to the point and not digress (*18*, p.116). Tracing a single line without a tremble in the hand from beginning to end (*18*, p.137), he should find no cause for including folklore, local colour, or landscape irrelevant to the characters (*18*, pp.64-68).

'A la deriva' is a near-perfect model: it begins immediately with the cause of a man's fatal injury and follows a single line of events through his early reactions, the steps taken to save his life, his physical deterioration, and his last thoughts, until the line is ended with the moment of his death. Although other stories can not match this for intensity, there is always a tendency for them to contain only the absolutely essential ingredients. Material that at first sight may appear extraneous usually proves on further consideration to serve a vital function. In the opening lines of 'La miel silvestre', for example, a reference to the narrator's cousins does not form part of Benincasa's story, but it does provide an indispensable warning and contrast. In 'El alambre de púa' — to take a different kind of example — the sequence of events is interrupted by a land-scape description when the horses have escaped through their third fence:

> ...en mansa felicidad prosiguieron su aventura. El día, en verdad, la favorecía. La bruma matinal de Misiones... etc.
> (p.74)

Since the horses' instinct to escape and roam at will is a part of the main theme, Quiroga needed to communicate some of the qualities in the countryside conducive to their yearnings. The day is young and fresh, full of promise, and the passage instils a mood of delight and adventure, surrounding the sense of freedom with an aura of beauty.

Among the pithy maxims listed in his 'Decálogo del perfecto cuentista' the fifth reads as follows: 'No empieces a escribir sin saber desde la primera palabra adonde vas. En un cuento bien logrado, las tres primeras líneas tienen casi la importancia de las tres últimas' (*18*, p.87). Determined to make the opening lines of his stories utterly relevant, pointing in exactly the right direction, he rarely begins with an introduction. As he once explained (*18*, p.62), his favourite opening is *ex abrupto*, since it gives the reader the impression that he knows part of the story, and then takes him by surprise by raising questions and showing his ignorance of the facts. In this way the reader's attention is claimed and his curiosity is aroused. More than half the *Cuentos de amor de locura y de muerte* begin *ex abrupto*, one of the best examples being 'Yaguaí': 'Ahora bien, no podía ser sino allí. Yaguaí olfateó la piedra — un sólido bloque de mineral de hierro — y dio una cautelosa vuelta en torno.' It is of course axiomatic in these openings that an event is already under way when the narrative uncovers its first points of reference. In this case the reader wishes to know who or what Yaguaí is, and what he is searching for. At the same time Quiroga establishes the point of view adopted in this story: the senses of his protagonist. He introduces the reader into the middle of an opening scene that illustrates the dog Yaguaí at his best and most contented. (In contrast to this effective opening it is worth noting the dull start of 'El solitario', which presents background information on the two protagonists before reaching the dramatic scenes.)

Only the ending of a story was — he believed — more important than the first lines. In his search for effective ways of closing a story he resorted to a variety of techniques, one of which was a short, pithy sentence:

> Pero Lidia no se asomó. ('Una estación de amor')
> Y cesó de respirar. ('A la deriva')
> Y me dormí. ('Nuestro primer cigarro')
> ¿Qué más puedo añadir? ('La meningitis y su sombra')

All are isolated lines whose abruptness endows the moment with emphatic finality: the end of the affair; the termination of a man's life; the close of an adventure; the culmination of a romance. Quiroga was well aware that this type of ending risked melodramatic or sentimental effects and joked that it was indispensable for rounding off stories of profound emotion (*18*, p.61). Although he illustrated this point by inventing amusing examples he might equally well have quoted the ending of his own story, 'La muerte de Isolda': '—No, no... ¡Es demasiado tarde!...'

One of the oldest tricks, the twist at the end of a story, was not ignored by Quiroga. The stories with the greatest contradictory effects at the end are probably 'El solitario', where Kassim's passivity does not prepare us for his sudden but calculated violence, and 'El almohadón de plumas', where Alicia's mental and physical deterioration lead us to expect her death but not the parasite in her pillow. Despite the success of such stories, however, Quiroga came to the conclusion that surprise effects draw excessive attention to the effects themselves, and that it is more difficult (and more satisfying) to write a good ending that is expected (*12*, II, p.62). He cited 'La meningitis y su sombra' as an example. In this story one of the chief devices used to maintain interest while fulfilling expectations was the repeated introduction of minor uncertainties: the narrator is unable to discern María Elvira's real feelings; the habit of pretence makes it difficult for them to distinguish between truth and role-playing; and the narrator's pride prevents — or at least delays — his open declaration of love. An even better example of this kind of ending, however, is 'A la deriva'. Although the protagonist's death looks inevitable (the powerful venom, the canoe drifting too slowly, the physical deterioration) there are three moments when he feels an improvement ('Se hallaba bien', 'El bienestar avanzaba', 'se sentía cada vez mejor') with the result that we share a little of his vain hope and therefore still receive an impact when we read the abrupt reminder: 'De pronto sintió que estaba helado hasta el pecho' (p.63). The death, though fully expected, then follows with poignancy. There are several variations of this technique of shielding a predictable outcome. Often an additional element is introduced to give the ending a small twist to the side (rather than a complete reversal). In 'La insolación' míster Jones's death is expected, but the dog's plight is not quite foreseen. In 'Yaguaí' our impending sense of disaster is fulfilled when the fox-terrier meets his death; but the ending itself turns away from the dog to show the impact on the family, especially the children, thereby increasing the emotional effect while indicating the human error involved.

In certain notable endings a strangely subdued effect is produced when action, high emotion, violence or horror are followed by a paragraph or two of calm, sometimes apparently detached, explanation or contemplation. It is worth recalling the macabre endings of 'El almohadón de plumas' and 'La miel silvestre' (which are discussed in Chapter 3), whose quasi-scientific information and cool language produce a secondary shock because of their callous indifference. In 'El alambre de púa' the episode leading to the bull's mutilation is followed by a brief summary of subsequent events, encouraging the reader's afterthoughts. 'Yaguaí', 'Los pescadores de vigas', and 'La meningitis y su sombra' represent different uses of this same technique of standing back to create a new perspective on the action, while offering an oblique commentary, before emotion has subsided.

One of the subsidiary effects of several endings is to indicate the irony underlying the events that have been narrated. As a general rule, situational irony occurs when a situation or event is described in a way that emphasizes the incongruities between appearances and reality. The victim appears to be mocked by the course of events, as though some force were taunting his confident innocence, an impression enhanced by the neatness of the way events arrange themselves.[21] A case of particularly cruel irony is 'La gallina degollada'. The Mazzinis, whose lives have been subjected to repeated blows by the illness of their boys, become blissfully joyful that their daughter is now safe from danger. Unknown to them, of course, their confidence is ill-founded, and the apparent safety of Bertita is a potentially dangerous situation. As though it were inevitable that their search for happiness should be thwarted, the creature dearest to them is killed. And Quiroga arranges events at the end with a special neatness so that the blow should occur on precisely the day when they have recovered from the latest false alarm about Bertita's health. Moreover, there is strong mockery implicit in the fact that the mad children should be the agents of the sane girl's death, and that madness should therefore triumph after all. Other cases of situational irony include the death of Yaguaí within yards of the safety of his home (after surviving months of hardship and danger) at the very hands of his unsuspecting owner; the murder of the jeweller's wife with the jewel that she covets, plunged near her bared breast as though it were a mocking substitute for a caress; and the ultimate fate of Barigüí, the bull whose bravado had previously reduced the two cautious horses to a ridiculous spectacle, to be converted into meat, some of which is carried home by the horse with the white forehead.

---

[21] See D.C. Muecke, *The Compass of Irony* (London: Methuen, 1969), and *Irony*, The Critical Idiom, 13 (London: Methuen, 1970). For a more comprehensive study of irony in Quiroga see my article (*32*).

The fact that in this last instance Quiroga adds the ironical information in an otherwise superfluous final sentence shows clearly that he was conscious of the effects that he was creating.

A measure of his technical success is the range of methods used to introduce variety and constantly renew the reader's interest. One of these is a careful and sparing use of scenes of dialogue, in which characters are brought to life, confrontations are highlighted, and tensions are dramatized. Another is the organization of the longer stories into phases and sections. The most interesting example, 'Una estación de amor', involves a system of overlapping subdivisions, some headed by numbers and others by seasons. A curious incongruity would be noticed by readers in Buenos Aires: the phase headed 'Verano' begins with the words 'El 13 de junio...', which is of course mid-winter in that part of the world. It is a clue to the fact that the four seasons in this story are determined not by external events but by the mood of the love affair, from its beginning in springtime, through its plenitude in summer to its degeneration in autumn and winter. The four numbered sections, on the other hand, loosely correspond to plot. A third technique, extremely effective in heightening tension, is the abrupt change of focus towards the end of a story. In 'Yaguaí', while the dog is scampering home the narrative leaves him and moves to Cooper's standpoint — a change which sharply increases our anxiety for the dog, partly because we can no longer follow Yaguaí's actions, and partly because we know something of which Cooper is unaware and are compelled to watch as he makes the mistake that we guess to be fatal. Other effective cases are 'La gallina degollada' (where the standpoint switches suddenly from the boys and Bertita to the blissfully unaware parents), 'El almohadón de plumas' (from Alicia to her husband and servant), 'La insolación' (from the dogs to míster Jones and back to the dogs), and 'La miel silvestre' (from Benincasa to his godfather).

Although in general Quiroga appears to have disliked the use of flashbacks, he did make effective use of foreshadowing. Three of the stories gain additional tension by this means. In 'La insolación' the dogs' two visions of death serve as indicators of the course that their master must avoid following; when we notice that he is embarking on that very course our involvement is all the greater. In 'La miel silvestre' the visit of *la corrección* during the night serves as a warning whose implications are fairly clear to the reader; when the novice Benincasa fails to act with caution he becomes the actor in a scene of dramatic irony. Perhaps the crucial instance of foreshadowing, however, is the killing of the hen in 'La gallina degollada', for it not only informs us of the children's delight at the sight of blood but directly influences their behaviour when Bertita interrupts their vision of the setting sun.

Point of view

With his emphasis on brevity, intensity, and the avoidance of ornament or digression, Quiroga was in fact seeking a unity of effect or impression.[22] There is consequently a tendency (though it is not an invariable practice) for him to adopt the point of view of a single character and to follow him or her through the story from beginning to end. Often this entails the exclusion of information explaining the thoughts or actions of other characters in the story. As we noticed in Chapter 2, 'Una estación de amor' narrates events so exclusively from Nébel's point of view that we know and see only what he knows and sees; it is only his thoughts and emotions that we observe intimately. At times the chosen standpoint is that of a group rather than an individual (five dogs, two *mensú*, two horses), but the effect is similar: a concentration of the reader's attention on those characters and a fuller involvement with their situation.

These effects are potentially greater, of course, in stories narrated in the first person. Five of the *Cuentos de amor de locura y de muerte* have first-person narrators (a slightly lower proportion than that found in Quiroga's overall production). One effect of this narrative form is the advantage offered to psychological insight. In 'Nuestro primer cigarro' the naïve

[22] As he must have been aware, Poe had considered that 'the unity of effect or impression is a point of the greatest importance' ('Nathaniel Hawthorne', in *The Works of Edgar Allan Poe* (Edinburgh: Adam & Charles Black, 1875), IV, p.215).

narrative, seemingly oblivious of the impact of events on other people, reminds us vividly of a child's mentality. While the narrator is in hiding, for instance, allowing the adults to believe him dead, there is no remorse for the distress he is causing his mother, but offended pride, envy, and the desire for revenge. An additional element here, however, is the intriguing self-analysis undertaken by a narrator who is — at the time of writing — a more mature person than the child he remembers. In other words, the narrator is simultaneously the eight-year-old protagonist and the benevolently ironical adult. A note of amusement and possibly also one of slight bitterness are perceptible in some of his words, with the result that we understand more profoundly the interrelation (sometimes of contrast, sometimes of mimicry) between the behaviour of children and that of adults. 'La meningitis y su sombra' offers a more straightforward case of first-person narrative. Although it is María Elvira who suffers the abnormal mental condition, our interest increasingly focuses on the confusion experienced by Durán. This is largely because in reporting the events in diary-like form, within hours of their incidence, he uses the very act of writing as a means of analysing and ordering his thoughts and emotions. The first-person narrative therefore becomes not merely a means of telling how Durán and María Elvira fall in love but a document charting psychological problems as they are actually developing.

In the other three stories the first-person narrators have a radically different function. It is illustrated in its simplest form by 'La miel silvestre'. The presence of a narrator is evident only in the first line — 'Tengo en el Salto Oriental dos primos' — after which the entire story is narrated in the third person. But two effects are irrevocable: firstly, that line endows the events with an air of authenticity; and secondly, it ensures that the story about Benincasa is always seen in relation to the brief episode concerning the narrator's two cousins. Rather than enlarge on this case here (since it is examined in Chapter 3), let us turn to the two more complex instances.

'Los buques suicidantes' has two first-person narrators whose material is arranged in such a way that we are told one story inside another:

Narrator A (pp.51-52) ———> Narrator B (pp.52-54) ———> Narrator A (p.54)

The outer story begins with introductory information in which
Narrator A sets the scene on a trans-Atlantic ship, where he and
other passengers have gathered to listen to the Captain's tales.
These listeners — particularly the young ladies — are shown to
be impressed by the Captain's experience. The passengers'
curiosity is aroused especially by the Captain's memory of discovering the deserted ship María Margarita. At this juncture one
of the passengers — a former sailor — tells his own story.
Although his words are presented to us via the original narrator,
to all intents and purposes we may regard him as a narrator in
his own right: Narrator B. His tale gives inside information
about one case of an abandoned ship: he is the sole surviving
member of a crew who one by one committed suicide by
jumping overboard. When he falls silent Narrator A resumes
control of the story, and during this final section some of the
unresolved issues are settled: the reasons for Narrator B's survival, the admirable quality of his feat, the relative plainness of
the Captain's own experience of abandoned ships. It is not difficult for us to perceive two principal effects achieved by this
narrative framework. Quiroga was dealing with a topic acknowledged throughout the world to be a mystery, and therefore one
reason for choosing first-person narrators was to counter-
balance anticipated disbelief with an impression of truthfulness.
The second effect concerns the relativity of the inner tale to the
story as a whole. Without its framework Narrator B's tale would
be little more than a bizarre episode. Within that framework,
however, it assumes the greater significance of a possible
explanation of one of the world's mysteries. Equally important
is the comparison that we are forced to make with the Captain's
tale. Like his impressionable passengers, we too find the
Captain's exploits eclipsed by the feat of that taciturn and
modest survivor.

Another story-within-a-story, 'La muerte de Isolda', has a
rather different development in which the second narrator's

material almost entirely assumes command over the external framework:

Narrator A (pp.35-36) ——→ Narrator B (pp.36-40) ——→
Narrator A (p.40: five lines) ——→ Narrator B (pp.40-42)

Once again, however, the chief purpose of the arrangement is to create a sense of relativity. Narrator A's own attraction to the woman at the opera means that he is in a sense a reduced image of Narrator B (Padilla) in terms of level of involvement, extent of loss, and intensity of emotion. Moreover, being younger and less experienced he is particularly capable of learning from the other man's error. Padilla's story therefore becomes not merely a sad tale but a lesson.

Narrative style

Quiroga's advice to a young poet in 1907 reveals a fastidious-ness about language rarely acknowledged by his critics: 'Ahora, joven poeta, te aconsejo que trabajes más tus versos. Si una elegante negligencia de amateur es linda, mucho más lindo es hacer versos completos para ti y todo el mundo' (*12*, II, p.58). It is a care that he himself carried over to his prose style. A com-parison of early and late versions of his stories shows clearly that he made copious amendments in search of clarity, precision and conciseness.[23] One characteristic complaint about his style was, in Guillermo de Torre's words: 'Escribía..., por momentos, una prosa que a fuerza de concisión resultaba confusa; a fuerza de desaliño, torpe y viciada.'[24] Yet whatever other reservations critics might have, there can be no justification for accusing him of negligence. Moreover, the so-called faultiness of his prose is itself a controversial matter. His collection *Cuentos de la selva (para niños)* was turned down as a school text in the 1920s on the grounds that it was not sufficiently correct, polished or

---

[23] See José Pereira Rodríguez, 'El estilo' (*19*, pp.183-206). Material made available to me in the Archivo Horacio Quiroga of the Biblioteca Nacional (Montevideo) confirms this impression.

[24] *Horacio Quiroga, Cuentos* (Madrid: Aguilar, 1950), Prólogo, p.19.

instructive (and, incidentally, its theme did not convey a moral). On the other hand his fellow Uruguayan, Emir Rodríguez Monegal, made the impeccably sound remark that if one takes as the standard of good writing the rules of the Real Academia Española in its grammar and dictionary then Quiroga did not write well; but if one's standards are effectiveness and the ability to express oneself with the maximum of energy, then he wrote well (*26*, pp.99-100).

One of the underlying issues here is the plainness of Quiroga's prose. Style was not for him an end in itself but a vehicle to serve his overall purpose. He mocked a friend for smoking a full cigarette before deciding in which order to place two adjectives, and a French writer for drinking three cups of coffee while choosing the word order for a single sentence (*18*, p.68). To his mind the writer's ideal should be 'el vehículo exclusivo de la intensidad: estilo sobrio y conciso...' (*18*, p.93). There should be no poetic embellishments, no search for musical effects, and no unnecessary adjectives (*18*, p.87).

In considering whether Quiroga obeyed his own maxims it is useful for us to notice that his style necessarily varied according to the nature of his material. To call it plain is, of course, to use a relative rather than an absolute term. Let us therefore take three excerpts from 'Yaguaí' as examples of different grades of prose style.

(i) La prueba, si no concluyente, desanimó a Cooper. Se olvidó luego de ello, mientras el *fox-terrier* continuaba cazando ratas, algún lagarto o zorro en su cueva, y lagartijas. (p.98)

In a context such as this short paragraph, where he is interested in presenting a bald statement of events or facts, Quiroga avoids any descriptive adjectives or adverbs, any metaphorical expressions, or any vocabulary that is not purely functional. His sentence structure is simple, even to the point where — as here — it merely links words in list-like fashion. Nothing distracts from the compact, clear reporting.

A dozen lines below this we find a paragraph where, summarizing Yaguaí's perception of the drought's effects, Quiroga chooses to add occasional affective elements:

(ii) El *fox-terrier* vivió desde entonces sentado bajo su naranjo, porque cuando el calor traspasa cierto límite razonable, los perros no respiran bien echados. Con la lengua de fuera y los ojos entornados, asistió a la muerte progresiva de cuanto era brotación primaveral. La huerta se perdió rápidamente. El maizal pasó del verde claro a una blancura amarillenta, y a fines de noviembre sólo quedaban de él columnitas truncas sobre la negrura desolada del rozado. La mandioca, heroica entre todas, resistía bien. (p.99)

The salient characteristic here too is the plain use of words. The adjectives are still sparse, three indicating literal facts: 'progresiva', 'primaveral', 'truncas'; two implying simple judgement: 'cierto', 'razonable'; and two referring to actual colour with a minimum of subjective impression: 'claro', 'amarillenta'. It is worth noting, however, that two are not entirely literal. The term 'desolada' is partly a hyperbolic treatment of the literal ('laid waste'), but partly too a word to convey the mood aroused by the sight ('joyless'). And 'heroica' serves purely to indicate the author's sentiment. Both adjectives are strictly unnecessary to the information imparted, but their inclusion shows Quiroga's desire to produce an intensifying effect by the simplest possible means. Although the paragraph is virtually devoid of metaphor, three expressions introduce figurative language in its most rudimentary form. In the first line 'vivió' has a mildly hyperbolic use. In the second sentence 'asistió a la muerte... de cuanto era brotación...' enhances a literal reality (the death of all young growth) by means of a slightly exaggerated reference to Yaguaí's constant presence. And in the sentence 'La huerta se perdió' the simple metaphor serves to imply precisely the owners' reaction to the loss of their produce. At one point Quiroga resorts to an unusually abstract formula: 'cuanto era brotación primaveral'. It is a compact expression, and this is no doubt one reason for its use. But the main purpose would appear to be that of evoking the feeling behind the concrete reality. The abstract noun 'brotación' helps him to emphasize the concept of newness and therefore to suggest how the death of things is rendered more poignant because they are still young. A final and extremely important feature to be noted in this paragraph is the extent to which — contrary to his normal practice — he has varied the number and position of subordinate clauses, and caused the overall length of sentences to fluctuate. This is not merely to avoid uniformity. The brevity of 'La huerta se perdió rápidamente' is contrived to emphasize the notion of speed, and clearly indicates the author's willingness to adapt style in support of meaning.

Not far below this passage occurs a paragraph which illustrates a third grade of prose style:

> (iii) Alrededor, cuanto abarcaban los ojos del *fox-terrier*: los bloques de hierro, el pedregullo volcánico, el monte mismo, danzaba, mareado de calor. Al Oeste, en el fondo del valle boscoso, hundido en la depresión de la doble sierra, el Paraná yacía, muerto a esa hora en su agua de cine, esperando la caída de la tarde para revivir. La atmósfera, entonces ligeramente ahumada hasta esa hora, se velaba al horizonte en denso vapor, tras el cual el sol, cayendo sobre el río, sosteníase asfixiado en perfecto círculo de sangre. Y mientras el viento cesaba por completo y en el aire, aun abrasado, *Yaguaí* arrastraba por la meseta su diminuta mancha blanca, las palmeras negras, recortándose inmóviles sobre el río cuajado en rubí, infundían en el paisaje una sensación de lujoso y sombrío oasis. (pp.99-100)

We are struck not only by the fact that the adjectives are more numerous, but that several of them have a figurative meaning: 'mareado', 'muerto', 'asfixiado', 'lujoso'. Although they do not excel in originality, the adjectival expression 'de cine' does stand out as an inventive way of indicating the uniform and unrippled surface of the water. Quiroga's increased attention to embellishment and feeling here is reflected in the fact that he twice uses combinations of adjectives, uncommon in a writer whose maxim was 'No adjetives sin necesidad' (*18*, p.87). Both cases have other features unusual for Quiroga. The first, 'diminuta mancha blanca', creates a periphrastic version of the word 'cuerpo' (which he would normally have preferred) whose purpose is to emphasize how the dog merges with and is dwarfed by his surroundings. In the second, 'lujoso y sombrío oasis', the effect of placing the adjectives in front of their noun is to enhance their affective value while reducing their descriptive function. The numerous metaphors, without being strikingly original, are carefully chosen to personify the rock ('danzaba, mareado'), the River Paraná ('yacía, muerto..., esperando... para revivir'), and the sun ('sosteníase asfixiado en perfecto círculo de sangre'), in an evident attempt to blur the distinction between Yaguaí's sensations or thoughts and the inanimate landscape. The heightened aesthetic inspiration of the author when he composed this paragraph led to the enclitic use of the reflexive pronoun in 'sosteníase' — an affectation common among *modernista* writers, but fairly uncommon in Quiroga's mature works. Possibly the most conspicuous feature of the passage, however, is the use of longer sentences, with subordinate clauses and phrases slowing the rhythm to a pace consistent with the drowsy scene. In a cumulative effect, sentences increase in length until the paragraph is rounded off with the most complex and extensive of all four. Quiroga delays its main clause, as though to ensure that the sensation of coolness that it refers to — in contrast with the heat that dominates the rest of the passage — should be reached only with a sense of relief at the end of a prolonged effort.

In *Cuentos de amor de locura y de muerte* Quiroga's prose style usually fluctuates between the first and second grades discussed above. The third and more consciously artistic level occurs in isolated paragraphs within a few of the stories, and the subject matter is almost invariably a landscape description.

Having qualified the view that Quiroga's prose style is always plain, let us consider the matter of regionalism, which according to critics like Raimundo Lazo (*8*, p.xxiv) abound in his stories. Aware of the prevailing mode among River Plate writers

Quiroga cautiously advocated 'el uso muy sobrio de la lengua nativa' (*13*, p.361). A comparison with contemporaries such as Ricardo Güiraldes (*Cuentos de muerte y de sangre*, 1915; *Don Segundo Sombra*, 1926) quickly reveals that he followed this guideline. He does include appropriate regional vocabulary to refer to trees, plants and animals typical of the area (*catiguá*, *tacuapí*, *urú*, etc.), and he occasionally uses Latin American terms where Peninsular Spanish alternatives exist (*carpición* for *desherbaje*, *yuyo* for *mala hierba*, etc.). But in all such cases the context makes the words either indispensable or else preferable to their Peninsular equivalents. Quiroga's caution is well illustrated by the way he actually explains the meaning of a local word in 'El alambre de púa': 'capuera — desmontante que ha rebrotado inextricable' (p.72). In general his style is not a deliberate reflection of local flavour. Even in the dialogue we notice that most characters other than *peones* use *tuteo* instead of *voseo* (which was the usual familiar form for most social classes in Argentina, though less prominent in Uruguay). His practice is well summarized by his own comment: 'Antes bien, en la expresión de cuatro o cinco giros locales y específicos, en alguna torsión de la sintaxis, en una forma verbal peregrina, es donde el escritor de buen gusto encuentra color suficiente para matizar con ellos, cuando convenga y a tiempo, la lengua normal en que todo puede expresarse' (*13*, p.361).

Although we noticed above that Quiroga saw sobriety and concision as hallmarks of intensity, his style tends at times towards a heightening of emotion, even towards hyperbole. Occasionally this effect is achieved through the use of exclamation marks, as when he refers to the Mazzinis' despair after their child becomes insane: '¡Luego su sangre, su amor estaban malditos! ¡Su amor sobre todo!' (p.45). More frequently the intensity is expressed through words, phrases or sentences representing extremes or completeness: 'Nébel llegó al más alto grado de pasión que puede alcanzar un romántico muchacho de dieciocho años...' (p.9); 'Viví en un segundo... el más adorable sueño de amor que haya tenido nunca' (p.35).[25]

---

[25] Nicolás A.S. Bratosevich uses the terms *hiperestesia* and *totalización* in his detailed study of the phenomenon (*20*).

Naturally, it is a stylistic trait in harmony with those scenes where the intention is to suggest profound emotion. But these sweeping expressions may appear whenever the circumstances are extreme. For example, while the *peones* at a timber site are working in appalling conditions to meet a deadline: 'Pero el tiempo proseguía cargando, sin el más ligero soplo' (p.112). Or while Candiyú fights the current to reach the shore with his log in tow: 'Hizo lo que jamás volverá a hacer nadie para salir...' (p.114).

A contrasting trait is Quiroga's sense of humour. It is noticeable, for example, when Nébel showers Lidia's carriage with streamers: 'Mas aquello llegaba ya a la falta de respeto a personas, cocheros y aun al carruaje: las serpentinas llovían sin cesar' (p.7). Usually the humour is one product of the author's gentle mockery of human behaviour, or else an indication that he is aware of the disproportion or incongruity of an event. When Nébel's adolescent inclination to extreme behaviour has caused him to load his revolver, for example, Quiroga inserts an amused parenthesis in the narrative: 'Pero un recuerdo lo detuvo: meses atrás había prometido a un dibujante alemán que antes de suicidarse un día — Nébel era adolescente — iría a verlo' (p.19). In one or two stories this attitude develops into a conspicuously ironical style. It is worth recalling that verbal irony is a use of words whose apparent meaning belies the real meaning; the author (or narrator) adopts a mask of sublime innocence which emphasizes the incongruity of his words, or else he uses the words at the expense of someone who is confidently unaware of their real meaning.[26] In the first two paragraphs of 'La miel silvestre' the two boys who disappear on an adventure are gently mocked through this kind of style:

> Tengo en el Salto Oriental dos primos, hoy hombres ya, que a sus doce años, y a consecuencia de profundas lecturas de Julio Verne, dieron en la rica empresa de abandonar su casa para ir a vivir al monte. Este queda a dos leguas de la ciudad. Allí vivirían primitivamente de la

[26] I am heavily influenced by D.C. Muecke for the terms used here, particularly in his *Irony*, The Critical Idiom, 13 (London: Methuen, 1970), pp.25-33.

caza y de la pesca. Cierto es que los dos muchachos no se
habían acordado particularmente de llevar escopetas ni
anzuelos; pero, de todos modos, el bosque estaba allí, con
su libertad como fuente de dicha y sus peligros como
encanto.

Desgraciadamente, al segundo día fueron hallados por
quienes los buscaban. Estaban bastante atónitos todavía,
no poco débiles, y con gran asombro de sus hermanos
menores — iniciados también en J. Verne — sabían aún
andar en dos pies y recordaban el habla. (p.115)

There is an incongruity about the boys' enterprise, through their
innocent failure to pay due attention to basic social custom or
their scorn for fundamental practical problems. Quiroga
encourages our sense of the absurdity of their action by
describing it as 'rica' — a word whose apparent meaning ('fine',
'lovely', 'delicious', etc.) contradicts our immediate perception
that the enterprise is extremely silly. It is a case of ironic anti-
phrasis. Three sentences later we reach a case of irony through
meiosis: 'no se habían acordado particularmente de llevar
escopetas ni anzuelos.' 'Particularmente' is clearly an under-
statement: what the boys above all needed to take was their guns
and fishing tackle, but Quiroga uses the word that represents
their innocent, unaware position, revealing the incongruity of
their lack of precaution. This mimicry — this imitation of the
boys' naïve attitude in order to show it to be out of place — is
repeated at the beginning of the second paragraph, where the
key word, 'desgraciadamente', is another instance of anti-
phrasis, belying the true opinion of the author ('afortunada-
mente').

It would be possible to extract further examples from this
passage, but the instances that I have cited are sufficient to make
the point that when it suited his purpose Quiroga was capable of
fairly heavy verbal irony. The opening page of 'Los pescadores
de vigas', and certain paragraphs in 'Una estación de amor' and
'La meningitis y su sombra', are further cases. Clearly this
feature of style is symptomatic of Quiroga's underlying ironic
perception of situations, events and human behaviour, and

therefore further evidence of the fact that style was not for him an end in itself but an implement whose function was to communicate efficiently.

Rather than languishing in a constant plainness — as a few detractors would have us believe — Quiroga's narrative prose sometimes acquires the necessary embellishments to evoke moods, temporarily incorporates local vocabulary and expressions, quite frequently resorts to hyperbolic and other intensifying methods, and often acts as the vehicle for humour and irony. However, it is admittedly not for his functional style but for his great skill with structural techniques that he is considered one of the masters of short story writing in Latin America. The abrupt openings, the rapid and concise developments, the devices for renewing and heightening tension, and the abundant variety of endings all serve him well in his artistic ambition to feel with intensity, communicate energetically, and hold the reader's attention (*18*, p.93).

8. Conclusion: the Universal Dimension

The three themes identified in the title *Cuentos de amor de locura y de muerte* are potentially psychological topics. Indeed, Quiroga explores the bewitching effect of physical attraction, the power of emotions, the failure to control destructive impulses, and the need to retain pure youthful memories. He traces pathological madness as a disease, as acts of violence, as passion, and as hallucinations. And he introduces us to the behaviour and thoughts of a dying man or — by contrast — a child's innocent lack of concern at the death of a relative. Despite the fantastic dimension to several of his tales, therefore, Quiroga should be taken seriously as an acute observer of the human psyche.[27] In making this claim, however, I am keeping in mind a fundamental point: that he proves more interested in human behaviour in its outward manifestations than in its psychological causes. His characters seldom analyse themselves, and he as author only occasionally undertakes an examination — as opposed to a mere citing — of their thoughts. Even insanity, though represented in broadly accurate symptoms, rarely becomes a focus of interest in its own right, serving chiefly to create sensational effects and unusual situations. Under the same conditions, several other aspects of human behaviour emerge as recurrent underlying themes.

It is clear that one of Quiroga's main interests was the moral strength of his protagonists: their acts of tenacity, fortitude, composure and heroism. The sole survivor from a ship's crew who have committed mass suicide, for example, reveals extraordinary modesty, coolness, and even nonchalance ('Los buques suicidantes'). In the case of a man bitten by a venomous snake

[27] Introducing an edition of *Cuentos de la selva (para niños)*, 4th ed., (Montevideo: C. García, 1943), p.20, Francis de Miomandre declared that Quiroga was 'sobre todo, de una extremada agudeza psicológica'. For most critics, however, any psychological depth found in Quiroga's stories derives mainly from what the fiction reveals about the author himself.

('A la deriva') we are struck by the rational assessment of his situation, the stoicism, the resoluteness, and the tenacious use of the utmost effort. And Candiyú ('Los pescadores de vigas') displays exceptional skill, physical strength and courage in defying the swollen waters of the river Paraná, though perhaps the feature of this story that most fascinated Quiroga was the man's willingness to expose himself to extreme danger for the sake of earning a gramophone (a luxury consumer good). It is not safe for us to assume that such behaviour is always presented as a model for us to follow, but it clearly does illustrate the human capacity to rise above the mediocre and to perform unusual feats.

Closely associated with this is the resourcefulness and self-sufficiency displayed by the various pioneers in Quiroga's stories. A striking case that comes to mind is that of Ramírez ('El alambre de púa'), who ingeniously arranges his barbed wire fence so that the persistent bull will be able to penetrate safely when under no pressure, but will gore itself on the barbs when attempting a hurried escape. The reader may be repelled by the result, but what this incident illustrates is the ability of the human settler to draw on his inner resources in order to protect his livelihood and thus survive in a difficult environment — and it is this that Quiroga admired. As we noticed in Chapter 5, the lives of pioneers are fraught with hardship and even occasionally exposed to danger. The human capacity for endurance is tested only under severe conditions, and many of his protagonists prove willing to submit themselves to these tests: the *mensú* fleeing in torrential rain from his employers, the log-hunter pitting himself against a river in flood, the sailors assuming control of a mysteriously abandoned ship.

While the search for adventure is treated as a natural instinct capable of bringing out admirable qualities in people, there are signs that Quiroga regarded in a negative light certain human tendencies allied to it. Imprudence and overconfidence bring disastrous consequences in 'La insolación' and 'La miel silvestre'. There are substantial differences, of course, between míster Jones and Benincasa, notably the vast experience of the former and the inexpertise of the other in the bush. What they have in common, however, is insufficient respect for the natural conditions. Whereas there is no suggestion that Paulino's death in 'A la deriva' could easily have been avoided (no focus, for example, on the idea that he might have been inattentive) there is a strong implication in the other two cases that more moderate behaviour would have prevented the fatal outcome.

One characteristic undoubtedly censured in several stories is pride. In 'Una estación de amor' insurmountable obstacles to the love between Nébel and Lidia are raised by the parents' obsessions with their public image and social status. A successful romance is almost impeded in 'La meningitis y su sombra' by Durán's wounded self-esteem (represented by the dream in which he is a mere *sombra*). This form of self-centredness is matched by the lack of consideration for other people illustrated in several of the tales. Eduardo's childish thoughtlessness makes him oblivious to his mother's grief in 'Nuestro primer cigarro', while a less easily pardonable case is Jordan's coldness to his bride in 'El almohadón de plumas'. At times the issue connects with the problems of employer-employee relationships, illustrated in the minor instance of míster Jones's inattentive or disobedient *peón* in 'La insolación', and the highly important instance of the harsh *mayordomo* in 'Los mensú', where this aspect of human behaviour is connected with social injustice.

It will be noticed that the characteristics now under discussion all produce destructive results in Quiroga's stories, and we may justifiably assume that the author regarded them as human weaknesses. Other failings that we observe in passing include addiction to drugs ('Una estación de amor') and to alcohol ('La insolación'); covetousness ('El solitario'); lack of willpower ('Los mensú', 'El almohadón de plumas', 'El solitario'); and a perverse self-destructiveness ('La muerte de Isolda', 'Los buques suicidantes').

Some critics take the view, with Raimundo Lazo, that the lasting quality in Quiroga's stories is 'lo humano universal en que el hombre se reconocerá siempre, con sus enigmas, sus proyectos, sus ansias y sus luchas a su paso por el mundo' (*8*, p.xxv). Noé Jitrik has emphasized one aspect in particular of the eternal human dimension: 'la ineptitud de los mejores

personaje de Quiroga para superar el aislamiento en que viven'
(*22*, p.110). In his opinion, Quiroga's own sense of solitude is
imparted to the fictional characters. Although his remarks convincingly apply to the collection *Los desterrados* and the
opening story of *El desierto* they do not at first seem particularly
appropriate to *Cuentos de amor de locura y de muerte*. In our
collection there is little attempt overtly to depict men suffering
from solitude, or indeed to comment on the human situation at
all. However, if we consider the common denominator of the
lives of most of the characters in the collection we inevitably
conclude that there is more than a grain of truth in Jitrik's
observation. We notice several cases of relative — if not
absolute — isolation: míster Jones, Kassim, Alicia, Paulino,
Rodríguez and Zaninski, Fragoso, Candiyú. In addition to these
characters there are many others whose lives are tragically
afflicted by adverse circumstances or events: Nébel and Lidia,
Padilla and Inés, the Mazzinis and their children, Cayetano and
Podeley, and Cooper and his family. And to all this we may add,
of course, the extensive range of unnatural and premature
deaths. In perspective, therefore, there is little to alleviate the
general impression that Quiroga's underlying view of the human
condition was essentially one of sadness, hardship, misfortune
and suffering.

It must be stressed, however, that the stories in this collection
do not attempt any philosophical presentation of this view. In
Chapter 7 I have attempted to show that the structure and style
of Quiroga's stories prove his sense of irony. By implying that
the world and human nature are full of contradictions, and by
showing a predilection for incidents suggesting the mocking
quality of life, he drew close to the metaphysical notion of
General Irony. But it is doubtful whether he was fully aware of
this. In his stories, certainly, he did not formulate the concept in
terms of the incongruity and absurdity of the human
predicament. The point is that although eternal issues always
underlie the *Cuentos de amor de locura y de muerte* and
frequently rise to the surface, the usual emphasis of the stories is
concrete rather than abstract. For this reason the majority of
critics have tended to regard Quiroga as primarily something

other than a universal author. There are those who, like Enrique
Anderson Imbert, think of him as 'the great narrator of
abnormal themes'.[28] But more typical views are those of Luis
Leal, who finds him 'el mejor representante del cuento criollo',
and Emir Rodríguez Monegal, who firmly believes that 'en el
juicio perdurable del lector se imponen sobre todo los relatos de
monte'.[29] It is reasonable to acknowledge that despite the
eternal human dimension his stories undoubtedly have,
Quiroga's personal hallmark was the artistic recreation of life in
Misiones.

[28] *Spanish-American Literature: A History* (Detroit: Wayne State Univ. Press,
1963), p.298.

[29] Leal, *El cuento hispanoamericano* (Buenos Aires: Centro Ed. de América
Latina, 1967), p.31. Rodríguez Monegal, *19*, p.18.

Index

Page numbers below refer to places in the Critical Guide where individual stories are mentioned or discussed.

Bibliographical Note

A. BIBLIOGRAPHY

Rela, Walter, *Horacio Quiroga. Repertorio bibliográfico anotado 1897-1971* (Buenos Aires: Casa Pardo, 1972). The list below omits all but the most essential items included in this indispensable work.

B. PRINCIPAL AVAILABLE COLLECTIONS OF QUIROGA'S STORIES

1. *Cuentos de amor de locura y de muerte* (1917) (Buenos Aires: Losada, 17th ed., 1981).
2. *El salvaje* (1920) (Buenos Aires: Losada, 3rd ed., 1976).
3. *Anaconda* (1921) (Buenos Aires: Losada, 5th ed., 1977).
4. *El desierto* (1924) (Buenos Aires: Losada, 5th ed., 1977).
5. *Los desterrados* (1926) (Buenos Aires: Losada, 7th ed., 1976).
6. *Más allá* (1935) (Buenos Aires: Losada, 4th ed., 1975).
7. *Horacio Quiroga: Cuentos escogidos*, ed. Jean Franco (Oxford: Pergamon, 1968). Vocabulary and notes for English readers, but unrepresentative selection (almost entirely Misiones stories).
8. *Horacio Quiroga: Cuentos*, ed. Raimundo Lazo (Mexico: Porrúa, 1977). Twenty-four stories embracing most periods and themes.
9. *Horacio Quiroga: Cuentos*, ed. Emir Rodríguez Monegal (Caracas: Biblioteca Ayacucho, 1981). Over 450 pages of stories, plus an introductory essay and a chronology. Expensive.

C. TRANSLATION

10. *The Decapitated Chicken and Other Stories*, translated by Margaret Sayers Peden (Austin: Univ. of Texas Press, 1976; repr. in paperback 1984).

D. BIOGRAPHY AND AUTOCRITICISM

11. Annie Boule-Christauflour, 'Horacio Quiroga cuenta su propia vida', *Bulletin Hispanique*, 77 (1975), 74-106. Takes account of letters in *12*, below.
12. *Cartas inéditas de Horacio Quiroga*, I: ed. Arturo Sergio Visca; II: ed. Mercedes Ramírez de Rossiello & Roberto Ibáñez (Montevideo: Instituto Nacional de Investigaciones y Archivos Literarios, 1959).
13. José M. Delgado & Alberto J. Brignole, *Vida y obra de Horacio Quiroga* (Montevideo: Claudio García, 1939). The best account, written

by two of Quiroga's friends. At times misleadingly based on short stories rather than facts.

14. La vida en Misiones, ed. Jorge Ruffinelli. Obras Inéditas y Desconocidas, 6 (Montevideo: Arca, 1969). Fascinating articles from magazines and newspapers.

15. Ezequiel Martínez Estrada, *El hermano Quiroga: cartas de Quiroga a Martínez Estrada* (Montevideo: Arca, 1968). Inside information about Quiroga's last years.

16. N. Baccino Ponce de León, *Horacio Quiroga: itinerarios* (Montevideo: Biblioteca Nacional, 1979). With many attractive photographs.

17. Emir Rodríguez Monegal, *Genio y figura de Horacio Quiroga* (Buenos Aires: Eudeba, 1967). Cf. *27.*

18. Sobre literatura, ed. Roberto Ibáñez. Obras Inéditas y Desconocidas, 7 (Montevideo: Arca, 1970). Includes newspaper articles on the art of the short story.

E. CRITICAL STUDIES

Books

19. Aproximaciones a Horacio Quiroga, ed. Angel Flores (Caracas: Monte Avila, 1976). Thirteen general articles and seven on individual stories (three from *Cuentos de amor de locura y de muerte*). Uneven, but important.

20. Nicolás A.S. Bratosevich, *El estilo de Horacio Quiroga en sus cuentos* (Madrid: Gredos, 1973). The best literary analysis to date, though patchy. Relates theme to style.

21. E. Espinosa, *Trayectoria de Horacio Quiroga* (Buenos Aires: Babel, 1980).

22. Noé Jitrik, *Horacio Quiroga: una obra de experiencia y riesgo* (Montevideo: Arca, 1967). The deepest study, linking life and literature.

23. ——, 'Horacio Quiroga, autor de folletines', in his *Ensayos y estudios de literatura argentina* (Buenos Aires: Galerna, 1970), pp.81-100. On Quiroga's fantasy serials published under the pseudonym Fragoso Lima.

24. J.L. Martínez Morales, *Horacio Quiroga: teoría y práctica del cuento* (Xalapa: Univ. Veracruzana, 1982).

25. María E. Rodés de Clérico & Ramón Bordoli Dolci, *Horacio Quiroga* (Montevideo: Arca, 1977). Very simple reading and explication of four stories, including 'El almohadón de plumas' and 'A la deriva'.

26. Emir Rodríguez Monegal, *Las raíces de Horacio Quiroga*. 2nd ed. (Montevideo: Editorial Alfa, 1961). Scholarly material, including the definitive arrangement of Quiroga's production into four phases.

27. ——, *El desterrado: vida y obra de Horacio Quiroga* (Buenos Aires: Losada, 1968). Contains brief commentaries on the stories, though they are difficult to locate. Important.

28. The Latin American Short Story: A Critical History, ed. Margaret

Sayers Peden (Boston: Twayne, 1983). Includes John S. Brushwood's brief 'Quiroga and the Basis of the Twentieth-Century Short Story'.

Articles

29. Jaime Alazraki, 'Un tema y tres cuentos de Horacio Quiroga', *Cuadernos Americanos*, 173, no.6 (1970), 194-205. On accidental death in 'El hijo', 'A la deriva', and 'El hombre muerto'.

30. ——, 'Relectura de Horacio Quiroga', in *El cuento hispanoamericano ante la crítica*, ed. Enrique Pupo-Walker (Madrid: Castalia, 1973), pp.64-80.

31. Manuel Antonio Arango, 'Sobre dos cuentos de Horacio Quiroga', *Thesaurus*, 37 (1982), 153-61. Briefly compares 'A la deriva' and 'El hombre muerto' on death, setting, and structure.

32. Peter R. Beardsell, 'Irony in the Stories of Horacio Quiroga', *Ibero-Amerikanisches Archiv*, 6, no.2 (1980), 95-116. Concentrates on 'La miel silvestre' and 'Van Houten'.

33. ——, 'The Psychological Element in Quiroga's Stories: Two Special Cases', *Spanish Studies*, 5 (1983), 1-12. On 'El conductor del rápido' and 'El hombre muerto'.

34. Annie Boule, 'Science et fiction dans les contes de Horacio Quiroga', *Bulletin Hispanique*, 72 (1970), 360-66. On 'El retrato' and 'El vampiro', showing Quiroga's imaginative use of scientific issues.

35. A. Chapman, 'Between Fire and Ice: A Theme in Jack London and Horacio Quiroga', *Symposium*, 24 (1970), 17-25. Disregard of heat in 'La insolación' and of cold in 'To Build a Fire'.

36. Mercedes Clarasó, 'Horacio Quiroga y el cine', *Revista Iberoamericana*, 45 (1979), 613-22. Suggests influences of the cinema on style and technique.

37. Mariano A. Feliciano Fabre, ed., 'Coloquio sobre Horacio Quiroga', *Revista de Estudios Hispánicos* (Puerto Rico), 6 (1979), 69-120. This includes articles by Juan José Beauchamp on social topics (85-120) and Ramón Luis Acevedo on Kipling and the animal stories (77-84).

38. Elsa K. Gambarini, 'El discurso y su transgresión: "El almohadón de plumas" de Horacio Quiroga', *Revista Iberoamericana*, 46 (1980), 443-57. On relationships between narrator, reader and characters.

39. César Leante, 'Horacio Quiroga: El juicio del futuro', *Cuadernos Hispanoamericanos*, 383 (1982), 367-80. Refutes the idea that Quiroga was a mere replica of Poe or Kipling.

40. Charles Param, 'Horacio Quiroga and his Exceptional Protagonists', *Hispania* (U.S.A.), 55 (1972), 429-35. On courage in eight stories, including 'Los pescadores de vigas'.

41. Daniel C. Scroggins, 'Vengeance with a Stick-pin', *Romance Notes*, 15 (1973-74), 47-51. Compares 'El solitario' favourably with stories by Barreto and García Calderón.

42. Edelweiss Serra, *Tipología del cuento literario: textos hispanoamericanos*

(Madrid: Cupsa, 1978). Includes a close textual analysis of 'La insolación'.

43. R.H. Shoemaker, 'El tema de la muerte en Quiroga', *Cuadernos Americanos*, 220, no.5 (1978), 248-64. A thoughtful study of 'A la deriva'.

44. P.G. Teodoresco, 'El camino de la ideología sociopolítica de Horacio Quiroga', *Ideologies & Literature*, 3, no.12 (March-May 1980), 16-24. Useful background to social themes.

CRITICAL GUIDES TO SPANISH TEXTS

Edited by
J.E. Varey and A.D. Deyermond